Spotlight on Young Children and the CREATIVE ARTS

Each issue of *Young Children*, NAEYC's award-winning journal, includes a cluster of articles on a topic of special interest and importance to the early childhood community. Most of the selections in this book originally appeared in *Young Children*, vol. 59, no. 4, in the cluster "Exploring the Creative Arts with Young Children." Ann S. Epstein's "Thinking about Art: Encouraging Art Appreciation in Early Childhood Settings" was originally published in *Young Children*, vol. 56, no. 3. Alice S. Honig's "The Language of Lullabies" is excerpted from an invited presentation at the annual meeting of the New York State Association for the Education of Young Children, New York City, March 2000.

Front cover photos: © Ellen B. Senisi.
Back cover photos: *(top)* © BmPorter/Don Franklin; *(bottom left)* © Ellen B. Senisi; *(bottom right)* © Walter F. Drew

Art samples displayed throughout are reproductions of original creations by young children.

National Association for the Education of Young Children
1313 L Street NW, Suite 500
Washington, DC 20005-4101
202-232-8777 or 800-424-2460

ISBN: 978-1-928896-23-1

NAEYC #286

Library of Congress Control Number 2005926793

Printed in the United States of America

Contents

Spotlight on Young Children and the *Creative Arts*

"Through arts education, very young children can experience nontraditional modes of learning that develop intrapersonal, interpersonal, spatial, kinesthetic, and logic abilities, skills, and knowledge, as well as traditional modes of learning that develop mathematical and linguistic abilities, skills, and knowledge. Because children learn in multiple ways, activities should reflect these multiple ways of knowing and doing."

From *Young Children and the Arts: Making Creative Connections,* a report of the Task Force on Children's Learning and the Arts: Birth to Age Eight (Washington, DC: Arts Education Partnership, 2000), 4.

A picture is worth a thousand words, so the introduction to this book on the creative arts will be brief to leave plenty of space for visual expressions of creativity. During the early childhood years, the creative arts curriculum typically includes activities that allow children to experience music, movement, dramatic play, puppetry, and the visual arts—painting, drawing, sculpting, and the use of other media; children make art *and* learn to appreciate the creative works of others.

The arts invite children to imagine, solve problems, express ideas and emotions, and make sense of their experiences. Creative arts are a meaningful part of the early childhood curriculum for their own sake and because they can enhance children's development of skills in literacy, science, mathematics, social studies, and more.

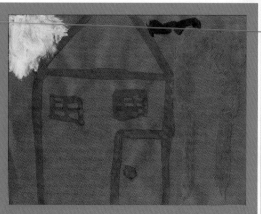

The collection of articles in this book presents a range of learning experiences that offer children multiple ways of knowing and doing. It begins with "The Language of Lullabies" as a reminder that nurturing creativity begins with babies. Author **Alice Sterling Honig** shares why it is important to sing lullabies with children, and she describes the various kinds of lullabies found in cultures throughout the world.

In "Sometimes a Smudge Is Just a Smudge, and Sometimes It's a Saber-Toothed Tiger: Learning and the Arts through the Ages," authors **Resa Matlock** and **John Hornstein** share numerous examples that "remind readers of the value of integrating play and the arts throughout the early childhood curriculum."

Corinna S. Bisgaier and **Triada Samaras,** authors with **Michele J. Russo** of "Young Children Try, Try Again: Using Wood, Glue, and Words to En-

hance Learning," describe a woodworking project that allowed children to express creativity and relate their artwork to their community, and enhanced their science, math, and literacy skills.

"Music Play: Creating Centers for Musical Play and Exploration," by **Kristen M. Kemple, Jacqueline J. Batey,** and **Lynn C. Hartle,** discusses the importance of planning opportunities for children to learn about music through play. The authors describe how to set up music centers that invite children to make musical discoveries.

In "Promoting Creativity for Life Using Open-Ended Materials," **Walter F. Drew** and **Baji Rankin** identify seven key principles for using open-ended materials in early childhood classrooms to promote spontaneous, creative expression and learning.

Linda Crane Mitchell, in "Making the MOST of Creativity in Activities for Young Children with Disabilities," provides a model for planning curricular activities that focuses on materials, objectives, space, and time. Using this model, teachers can be sure they support all children's creative expression.

"Music from Inside Out—Promoting Emergent Composition with Young Children," by **Jennifer Ohman-Rodriguez,** challenges teachers to foster children's emergent music-composing abilities, thereby allowing young children to be "music insiders."

"Education Is a Moving Experience: Get Movin'!" by perennially creative **Mimi Brodsky Chenfeld,** reminds readers that movement and dance are important parts of the curriculum and that "all concepts, topics, and themes have countless built-in dimensions of learning."

In "Thinking about Art: Encouraging Art Appreciation in Early Childhood Settings," **Ann S. Epstein** invites early childhood practitioners to expand art education to include style and aesthetics, artists' intentions, and the feelings art evokes. She presents language for talking about art and tips for including art appreciation in the curriculum.

— *Derry Koralek*

The Language of *Lullabies*

Alice Sterling Honig

Lullabies are a special kind of song. Across centuries and across cultures, caregivers have created these songs and melodies to calm young children and to soothe them into slumber. Learning music and words and combining them with hand and body motions is a wonderful way to wire children's brain connections for learning as well as bring them pleasure (Honig 1995).

Lullabies help young children relax. Their bodies sink into that somatic certainty of feeling safe and well cared for that allows children to let go of tensions and drift into sleep. The soothing melodies and rhythms are almost hypnotic. Quiet stanzas repeat over and over, with an endearing and enduring familiarity that reassures and comforts children.

Lullabies can be learned from grandparents and other family members and from music recordings like *Pillow Full of Wishes*, an audio CD by Cathy Fink and Marcy Marxer. The *New York Times* cited *Ninna Nanna: 1450–2002,* a collection of lullabies through the ages, sung by soprano Montserrat Figueras, as one of the finest classical CD recordings of 2003. Lullabies can be learned from books as a caregiver picks out the simple melody on a piano, guitar, or other instrument and then shares the song with babies. Lullaby words may vary, since the songs often are ancient and their origins lost over time. Some modern lullabies soothe with melody and rhythm without words.

Babies do not care in which language you sing a lullaby! They settle down if the melody is soothing and gentle and repetitive. They love to hear the same familiar treasured songs over and over. Although the goal of all lullabies is the same—to soothe babies—some have obscure or dark themes, so teachers may want to think about which lullabies they sing.

Lullabies provide a rich resource for enhancing multicultural breadth in an early childhood program. Teachers can sing lullabies daily with all the children, from the tiniest babies to kindergarten children who still need rest times. You can invite family members to come in and share lullabies from their culture with the class. A teacher's willingness to learn lullabies from other lands is a welcome sign for families of the acceptance and appreciation of their culture.

Alice Sterling Honig, PhD, professor emerita of child development at Syracuse University in New York, annually conducts the Quality Infant/Toddler Caregiving Workshop. More than 400 of her articles have been published. The books she has authored include *Playtime Learning Games for Young Children* and *Secure Relationships.*

Varieties of lullaby themes

The words of lullabies sometimes reveal the singer's feelings about life. They reflect many different impulses of the heart and soul, although the predominant theme expresses tenderness and deep love for the baby. Here are some of the variant longings, worries, wishes, and rejoicings woven into the words of lullabies from different cultures.

Tenderness

Tenderness is the message of most lullabies. At times the singer makes heroic efforts to consider the baby blameless, despite adult fatigue and long efforts to lull the child to sleep. The Argentine lullaby *"Arroro mi nino, arroro mi sol"* (Lullaby, my little child, lullaby, my sunshine) reassures the listener that the baby really wants to sleep, but that naughty dream just won't come; and even when baby closes his darling little eyes, they just open again! It is the dreams that are naughty, not the baby. This song ends with a special burst of love and a prayer that angels sent by God will protect the baby.

© Marilyn Nolt

Promising treats and sweets

Lullabies often promise treats or sweets for the child who will fall soundly asleep. The African American lullaby that begins "Hush, little baby, don't say a word, / Papa's going to buy you a mockingbird" makes a series of promises—"Papa's going to buy you a diamond ring," a looking glass, a billy goat, and so on—before closing with "If that horse and cart fall down, / You'll still be the sweetest baby in town!"

In the Yiddish lullaby *"Rozhinkes mit mandlen"* (Raisins and almonds), a mother sings about a snowy white goat who trots to market to get raisins and almonds for the baby. The older sister tending the cradle in the French lullaby, *"Fais dodo, Colas, mon petit frère"* (Go sleepy-sleep, Colas, my little brother), soothingly reassures her younger sibling that Mama is upstairs baking him a cake and Papa is downstairs making him hot chocolate. A Chinese lullaby promises boiled mutton for the baby when he wakes (Wilder & Engvick 1965). An African American lullaby tells a sleepy baby, "When you wake, you shall have all the pretty little horses."

Narrative stories in lullabies

When children grow from infancy into early childhood, soothing songs (not specifically created as cradlesongs) still help settle them at naptime. Long narrative songs, when sung softly over and over, help children slowly quiet down to listen to a familiar tale. Creative teachers can use imagination and ingenuity to create additional rhyming couplets. Some long narra-

tives have a scary verse toward the end, and it may be advisable to make up another ending.

An ancient Korean song about a green bird has no specific request for the child to go to sleep. Yet the soothing repetitive melody has served for centuries as a well-known lullaby. The narrator in "Old Bird, Old Bird" pleads with the bird not to sit down on the *noktu* bush. For if the noktu flowers fall to the ground, there will be no beans and then the bean curd seller will go away crying (Commins 2000).

Conjuring beautiful images

Teachers may want to choose lullabies for older children at rest time because of the beautiful imagery as well as the narrative interest of a song. Consider the charming animal imagery in the lullaby "Where Do You Sleep?"

The green worm sleeps in silk; the turtle sleeps in sand.

And the bluebird sleeps in a feather bed; the yak prefers to stand.

The white lamb sleeps in wool; the ermine sleeps in fur.

But the monkey sleeps in his mommy's arms, all warm and close to her! (Wilder & Engvick 1965, 26)

Ira Gershwin's "Summertime" from his opera *Porgy and Bess*—"Summertime and the living is easy, / Fish are jumping, and the cotton is high"—can be a wonderfully reassuring lullaby. Children drift into sleep hearing the magical words, "One of these mornings you're going to rise up singing, / Then you'll spread your wings and take to the sky. / But till that morning, there is nothing can harm you, with Mama and Papa standing by!"

Conclusion

Choose a variety of lullabies to send young children off to dreamland. Be adventuresome! Try songs in different languages. Do sing the same songs in gentle rhythms over and over in soothing low tones. When you are rubbing a toddler's back and quietly singing just for her, embroider the child's name into the melody. Sing folk tunes that specifically mention how precious children are. Add verses of your own to personalize a song for a child. Who knows, perhaps someday your verses will become part of the folklore of lullabies that others sing! As you sing in murmuring tones, let the lullaby soothe your soul and bring you peacefulness too.

References

Commins, D.B. 2000. *Lullabies of the world.* New York: Random House. (Music and words, with translations into English, for dozens of folk lullabies from many countries.)

Honig, A.S. 1995. Singing with infants and toddlers. *Young Children* 50 (5): 72–78.

Wilder, A., & W. Engvick. 1965. *Lullabies and night songs.* New York: HarperCollins. (Words and music for piano. Revised edition in press.)

Sometimes a **Smudge** Is Just a **Smudge**, and Sometimes It's a . . .

Saber-Toothed Tiger

Learning and the Arts through the Ages

Resa Matlock and John Hornstein

Adults who spend time playing with, talking to, or thinking about young children, react and express themselves as differently as the blind men of Indostan. Upon encountering an elephant, the first man patted the animal's sturdy side and exclaimed, "It's a wall!" "No, it's a spear," said another, feeling the tusk. The one who held the trunk was sure the elephant was like a snake. "No," said the man who touched an ear, "it is a fan." "A tree," pronounced the man touching the knee. And the one holding the tail was convinced it was a rope.

For teachers and parents attempting to make sense of what research tells us about how children learn to think and solve problems creatively, it can be helpful to remember that from Peoria to Indostan, humans are programmed to make sense of confusing data by turning them into stories (Bruner 1990). Stories stimulate not just the imagination but also our ability to organize a range of material into coherent units that make sense on an emotional and rational level (Egan 1988).

When you're four, as was Kalieb on the day he dictated the following, you might string your units together like this:

I took myself for a walk for a while and I found a snail who was right in the road and I saw a truck coming and then I saved him. And then we went for a walk and he had feet and he talked. And he had hands and eyeballs. And then we went home and started playing. Then that's it.

But these days, if you're teaching 4-year-olds, or 14- or 40-year-olds, and if you know the value of integrating play and the arts

Resa Matlock is a codirector of The Child Care Collection at Ball State University. The Child Care Collection, with the help of the Wolf Trap Foundation for the Performing Arts, is producing three training videos to document ways in which the arts can help young children learn self-regulation, improve their communication skills, and become more adept at making friends and getting along with peers.

John Hornstein, EdD, is an assistant professor in early childhood education at the University of New Hampshire and a research associate at Children's Hospital in Boston. His research focus is emotional development in young children. He helped develop the Touchpoints program based on the work of Dr. T. Berry-Brazelton, which combines relationship building and child development in a framework that professionals can use to enhance their work with families.

Photos © Ellen B. Senisi.

throughout the early childhood curriculum and life, your story might sound like this:

Once upon a time, long, long ago, many men, women, and children lived happily in cliffside caves carved by rain and wind. The men and women were of many different shapes and sizes, and the children were mostly small and noisy.

One day a hunting party limped home with thorns in their toes. Half of them whimpered in pain; the other half tried to remove the thorns while comforting the suffering hunters.

On this rainy afternoon the children ran in and out of the caves, dripping drops, tracking mud, and singing songs about old men snoring. One of the children, Culpepper, slipped and fell into the cold ashes from the previous night's campfire. Anvil, the father with the largest thorn in his biggest toe, bellowed, "You kids get out of here right now, or I'll feed you to the saber-toothed tigers!"

The children fled, all except for Culpepper. As he struggled to get to his feet, he bumped into a wall, leaving a smudge of charcoal. Something about the smudge looked familiar, as though a shadow had stuck around, even after the fire went out. It dawned on Culpepper that the smudge looked just like a mouse. "Hey!" he cried. "Look what I made!"

Palopeknee was so preoccupied tending to Anvil's toe that she failed to find any charm in the smudge. "Just wait till I show your father what you did to the wall," she yelled.

Culpepper scurried out the door. When he caught up with the rest of the group, Plinth noticed the black footprints that had followed him along the path. "Look what you made with your feet!" she exclaimed.

A sudden downpour obliterated the tracks, but not before Culpepper's brain made a lightning-like connection between shadows, smudges, and footprints. The drenched children ran for their play cave, where Culpepper told the others about the mouse he had made. The group's collective mind needed only seconds to embrace this new concept, and soon the children were daubing stories on the walls of the cave with mud and crushed berries as well as ashes. An hour later the walls were covered with black and purple handprints and footprints and smudges from elbows and knees.

In the midst of all the clamor and joy, one child suddenly stopped in mid-drawing. "A saber-toothed tiger! I made a saber-toothed tiger!"

The drawing and footprinting and smudging came to an abrupt halt. A tiger in the cave? Surely that was too dangerous! A sense of uneasiness spread through the children, and soon the youngest was crying and calling for his mother. The older

children were unable to console him, so they all ran off to the main cave to find their parents.

That night around the evening fire, after the hunting party had danced and sung the Hunt Dance and choreographed a new Toe Thorn Trot, the children told the story of the images they had made. The adults, now blessedly thorn free and able to process new information, recognized at once that the children had stumbled upon an exciting way to share joyful experiences and make meaning of unsettling encounters.

An age-old tool

Humans have always used the arts to share and make sense of their deepest joys and fears. When we bring the shadows out of the caves and turn them into story, dance, song, or picture, we transform our emotions into something to share with others. And on those rare days when all the planets are perfectly aligned, we react in ways that lead to a greater understanding for all.

We begin asking questions at a very early age, and the search for answers goes on until we die. Why am I here? How powerful am I? What am I capable of? Do you really love me? Do you see what I see? Will you still love me if I draw on the walls? Why are there monsters? Can you make them go away and not come back until I'm ready?

In 2004, many thousands of years after that first mouse smudge, adults are still trying to help themselves and children make sense of the world—to come to grips with the joyful and the unsettling. As researchers like Gardner (1982) remind us, the best way to help children process their lives is *not* by insisting that they sit quietly and passively.

Some of us accept that messiness and inappropriate behavior have meaning and realize that children's most important play and stories often include troubling and perplexing actions and ideas (Bruner 1990). Others of us, wanting to keep children safe and healthy, often try to eliminate trouble and perplexity. But sometimes the stories that help all of us grow *are* disturbing. If we want children to develop the capacity to find new, creative solutions, we must constantly search for ways to manage, even embrace, the disturbing parts of life.

Integrating the arts

The arts play a critical role in the human need for self-expression, for sharing thoughts and ideas, and for challenging old ways of thinking. One organization that supports early childhood professionals in their attempts to help children make sense of the world is the

> ## More on the Wolf Trap Institute . . .
>
> **Wolf Trap Institute for Early Learning Through the Arts** was founded in 1981. The institute provides arts-in-education services for children ages three through five and their teachers and families. Collaborations between performing artists and early childhood professionals are designed to enrich and motivate teachers' professional development and engage young children in active, creative learning experiences. For more information, visit www.wolftrap.org/institute.

> **T**he arts play a critical role in the human need for self-expression, for sharing thoughts and ideas, and for challenging old ways of thinking.

Wolf Trap Institute for Early Learning Through the Arts (see below, left, for more information).

Now that we are out of the cave, let's peek into a preschool classroom where a Wolf Trap teaching artist is visiting. Lorena Racanelli, a professional dancer, is dancing and singing with the children.

"Good morning, toes," she sings.
"Good morning, toes," the 19 children reply. Some of them can sing in tune; some cannot. All of them know how to move, although some prefer to first observe and give their movements some thought.

The drum-filled song chosen for the warm-up activity has a compelling beat. Most of the children join in willingly, even when Lorena asks them to lie down on their backs, stick their feet in the air, and pretend to pedal their bicycles.

"Good morning, bottom," sings Lorena.
"Good morning, bottom," echo the children.
The adults sitting around the room are a tad ambivalent. You can almost hear them thinking: "Movement—what a wonderful way for children to engage their bodies and minds, but I'm pretty sure I can no longer do the bicycle pedal."

Those of us who care for young children are concerned about many things, not the least of which is whether we can still do the bicycle pedal. By the time we reach a certain age, we have fewer synapses in our brains than when we were four, and we have devised a system of shortcuts to get us through each day. These shortcuts, especially for adults who work with or around large groups of children, often seem to be all that stand between the children and terrible consequences. "Stop!" is all we have time to get out before it's too late: Sally has already pushed Kanisha off the climber, and Ben has bumped into Abdul while running past him. We inquire sternly, "What were you thinking?" but the answers children give tend to involve saber-toothed tigers, dancing mice, and robots that sprout pogo sticks that allow them to leap buildings in a single bound.

We adults who are committed to finding more creative ways to help children consider their thoughts and actions might want to spend a day with Sean Layne, another Wolf Trap Institute teaching artist. A professional actor and director, Sean tells a story in which the

word *fierce* appears, then helps the children explore the meanings of the word.

"OK, my friends, let's see what we have in our shoes. Can anyone find a *fierce* face in his shoe and put it on to show his friends?"

Of course every child has such a face in his shoe, and hissing and growling ensue until Sean waves his magic wand and asks the children to look for a *quiet* face.

Steve Elm is a teaching artist with the New York City Wolf Trap Institute's creative arts team. He and his colleagues devise creative ways to use stories and drama to help young children develop critical problem-solving and thinking skills.

As the children try to decide whether to be enraged or overjoyed at the trick that Steve ("Sangura") has played on "Bui Bui," the spider that used to be their teacher, the spider/teacher has an epiphany: Lugging an imaginary bag of rabbit costumes into circle time can transform the classroom into an engaging universe where social and educational issues can be explored in ways that allow children to discover for themselves how their actions affect others.

Preschoolers know they can talk to their toes. When adults endorse that belief, children are free to explore powerful ideas as well as silly, fun ideas. Little twists in thinking or perception are what push humans into what we call *creativity*. Adult artists strive to maintain the freedom of thought that is natural to the preschooler. For all of us who manage to keep the creative windows open, helping children identify and expand odd connections is a powerful tool for making sense of daily life.

Sharing the wonder

Art with children works best when adults share in the discoveries. Teachers must bring their own curiosity and awe into the classroom and be prepared to acknowledge that children often lead in the discovery. One ongoing challenge is learning to recognize the moment of engagement, to embrace that physical and psychological place in which adults and children are free to make discoveries, and to look for opportunities to use materials in new ways.

Creative acts incorporate previous learning and experiences as well as new expressions. The surprise of

> **C**reative acts incorporate **previous learning and experiences** as well as **new expressions.**

Creative, Arts-Based Activities for Teachers to Consider

Use stories to make any activity more interesting. For example, before children begin an active, structured movement activity, tell a story to help them remember the warm-up sequence.

Use drama to help children think about issues such as anger management, conflict resolution, or respect for self and others. Invite children to make changes in the story's direction and outcome. For example, for a story in which someone's feelings have been hurt, one group of children may decide that an "I'm sorry" is needed, along with an offering of pretend candy and flowers. Another group might decide to spend its choice time making heart-covered cards for the person whose feelings were hurt.

Solicit children's input for every activity you plan. If you are making an obstacle course for the gross motor area, ask children what objects they would add. Is there a story that explains why the brown bear is in the cardboard tunnel? Can they make up a song to help everyone remember to hop on one foot three times before they crawl into the tunnel, just to make sure the bear is awake?

Learn to improvise well. This will allow any classroom event to become an occasion for learning. Children's play is a collectively produced, improvised activity. Consider taking a workshop or class in improvisation. You can learn basic performance and improvisational skills and use them to create a collaborative classroom environment in which everyone can take risks, think on their feet, and exceed their own expectations.

Encourage imagination. Props are a lot of fun, until you run out of places to store them. Imaginary bags of rabbit teeth, paws, noses, and whiskers take up a lot less room.

Offer new building materials.* Provide cardboard cartons and tubes, index cards, molding clay, and wood scraps instead of the blocks that the children have been playing with for months. Create a house or town. What about a bridge?

Play music to stimulate children's thinking. Observe the differences between the drawings children do while listening to a violin solo and ones they make while listening to Raffi singing "Baby Beluga in the Deep Blue Sea."

Make language portable. Has the sign that says "Wall" been hanging in the same place for more than six months? Ask the children to find a new place for it. Write the words of a simple poem on pieces of paper and have the children line up the words to make a different poem.

Let children experiment with movement or sound as a means of communication.* Can they send messages by drumbeat? With movements they make up and then combine to make a sentence? How difficult is it for their friends to understand them?

Teach creative problem solving.* Use two paper plates and some ping-pong balls. Ask the children to look for items in the room that they can use to move the balls from one plate to the other without touching them with their fingers. What will they think of, besides drinking straws, masking tape, string, or pipe cleaners?

* These activities adapted from *Project Spectrum: Early Learning Activities*, edited by Jie-Qi Chen (New York: Teachers College Press, © 1998 by Teachers College Press, Columbia University), 37, 123, & 46.

peekaboo leads to the discovery of a mouse smudge on the wall and ultimately to inventions that can change the way we all live. The willingness of adults to consider new ideas allows children to enter magical rooms where new ideas sprout springs and wings and begin to bounce and fly. Through interactions between children and adults, both in the home and in the classroom, one generation builds a legacy for the next, and we all contribute to a changing culture (Rogoff 1990).

Exploring emotion and context

Emotion and context, inside us and thousands of miles away from us, work together. Weather researchers recently noted that Edvard Munch painted *The Scream* after witnessing terrifying atmospheric effects in Norway following the eruption of Krakatoa volcano in Indonesia in 1883 (Radford 2003). A seismic occurrence on the opposite side of the globe prompted one of the most striking creative statements in history. Through art we find meaning in the interactions between emotion and context. For children struggling to understand a smudge, a shadow, the television news, or parent fears, arts-based activities can provide the means to make sense of the emotions and context (Gross & Clemens 2002).

> **T**rusting children with each other, without trying to control their discoveries, yields a richness rarely achieved when children work alone or under close adult supervision.

Creativity is often social. Culpepper's discovery of the mouse smudge became far more meaningful when he shared it with his peers. It became the means by which the children addressed their fears about saber-toothed tigers. Trusting children with each other, without trying to control their discoveries, yields a richness rarely achieved when children work alone or under close adult supervision (Paley 1981).

Early humans sensed the connection between creativity and meaning making. But they perhaps were not fully aware of how art can go beyond a prescriptive use of basic materials to a place where tomorrow's leaders first experiment with ways of addressing fundamental questions about individual identity and what it means to live in harmony with other people.

Conclusion

Saber-toothed tigers and terrorists, Legos and missions to Mars, children and adults solving problems and discovering new worlds: the work of learning in early childhood settings involves far more than providing developmentally appropriate materials or teaching pre-academic skills. It maintains intellectual possibility and emotional connections (Egan 1988). It involves—today and all over again tomorrow—children and adults working, playing, and thinking together, struggling to face real and imaginary joys and fears, sharing exciting discoveries and disappointing dead ends, with the help of pen and paper, music and movement, and story, song, and dance.

References

Bruner, J. 1990. *Acts of meaning.* Cambridge, MA: Harvard University Press.

Egan, K. 1988. *Primary understanding: Education in early childhood.* New York: Routledge.

Gardner, H. 1982. *Art, mind, and brain.* New York: Basic.

Gross, T., & S. Clemens. 2002. Painting a tragedy: Young children process the events of September 11. *Young Children* 57 (3): 44–51.

Paley, V. 1981. *Wally's stories.* Cambridge, MA: Harvard University Press.

Radford, T. 2003. Stratospheric echo locates Munch's "The Scream." *The Guardian,* December 10, 2003. Online: www.guardian.co.uk/international/story/0,3604,1103585,00.html.

Rogoff, B. 1990. *Apprenticeship in thinking: Cognitive development in social context.* New York: Oxford University Press.

Young Children Try, Try Again

Using *Wood, Glue,* and *Words* to Enhance Learning

Corinna S. Bisgaier and Triada Samaras, with Michele J. Russo

Corinna S. Bisgaier, MA, is the education director at Young Audiences of New Jersey in Princeton. She is a former English teacher who believes in the power of the arts to transform the learning environment. Corinna works to bring artists into partnerships with schools across New Jersey.

Triada Samaras, MA, is a teaching artist and mentor for Young Audiences of New Jersey, Studio in a School, and Artsgenesis. She holds a diploma and fifth year certificate from the School of the Museum of Fine Arts in Boston.

Michele J. Russo, BA, is the early childhood project coordinator for Young Audiences of New Jersey. Michele is a former Montessori school teacher assistant; she now coordinates and facilitates all early learning residencies in the Creative Beginnings program.

Photos © Michele J. Russo.

During a wood sculpture residency, Ms. Soto, the teaching artist in a preschool classroom, has a profound experience with a child prone to aggressive behavior. Spending time with Phillip as he builds his sculpture, Ms. Soto sees the child's tender and sensitive side. Phillip makes a sculpture of himself sitting on his roof watching the sun go down. He creates a chair out of cardboard and makes a sculpture of a person seated in it. With a delicate wash of watercolor painted over the whole sculpture, he represents the reflection of the sunset on his apartment building, which he calls "the sun all around."

uilding sculptures from wood blocks, shapes, knobs, and scraps is a process that is easily explored in the classroom, rich with learning opportunities, and highly engaging for children. It allows children to learn new skills and the dispositions needed to create a work of art. Through a wood sculpture unit, children may learn the names of local trees; the different leaves, acorns, pinecones, and seeds that each tree produces; the types and colors of wood; the softness or hardness of wood from various trees; the customary uses of wood in our culture; a wood's suitability for sculpture or wood carving; the names of artists who use wood in their artwork. Opportunities abound for the teacher to help children make connections between their artwork and the world around them, relating the project to key curriculum areas such as science, math, and literacy while children develop as creative artists.

Artists in early childhood classrooms

To help early childhood teachers integrate the arts in their classrooms, Young Audiences of New Jersey implemented the Creative Beginnings program in 1997 in the traditionally underserved cities of Newark and Trenton,

New Jersey. The program grew from an awareness that young children learn through play and that many early childhood teachers are no longer trained in the arts. Because of this gap between the teachers and the learners, Young Audiences of New Jersey saw an opportunity to forge partnerships between early childhood education centers and professional artists with backgrounds in early learning. These ongoing partnerships have demonstrated the power of the arts to make a difference in children's lives.

In the Creative Beginnings program, artists work with preschool children and provide teachers with tools to bring the arts into their classrooms. One artist, coauthor Triada Samaras, who trained at Studio in a School in New York City and at Teachers College, Columbia University, focuses on helping teachers lead the children through a unit on building wood block sculptures. Artists model teaching methods, strategies, and language for teachers. Many of the skills teachers learn can be adapted to uses besides art projects.

Teachers may incorporate a wood block sculpture project for a week or several months, depending on their comfort with the process. Children enjoy the project no matter how much time is given to it because, as Loris Malaguzzi writes in *The Hundred Languages of Children,* children have "surprising and extraordinary strengths and capabilities linked with an inexhaustible need for expression and realization" (Edwards, Gandini, & Forman 1998, 72).

To facilitate a wood block sculpture unit in the classroom, there are two areas to focus on: organizing the process and using language appropriately. Both areas are integral to maximizing children's learning.

Organizing the process

In planning a wood block sculpture project, consider ways to tie the unit to other learning taking place in the class. Begin with the simplest, most obvious connections. For example, how do the shapes of the wood pieces reinforce the math curriculum? Can the children find circles, squares, ovals, rectangles, hexagons, and other polygons in the wood scrap bin? What shapes result when two or more blocks are combined? Connect the shape search to the larger environment outside the school. Does a nearby building have interesting configurations of shapes? Does its architecture use wood in an interesting way? The sculpture

Explore resources in the community, such as nearby parks, churches, or buildings with interesting architecture.

project provides an opportunity for children to explore resources in the community, such as nearby parks, churches, or buildings with interesting architecture.

Adjacent to Bethany Academy in Newark, for example, an unusual wood structure modeled after an African hut adorns the roof of a church. It was both a visual and cultural point of departure for children. The hut sparked children's interest in African art. Viewing a small collection of African scuptures, the children were fascinated by the fertility figures. They discussed the sculptures and learned about their meaning, then drew their own figures. This classroom connection to learning—not only about simple math concepts through a wood sculpture unit but also about neighborhood architecture, trees, wood, and art—makes the wood unit come alive in a unique way in each classroom.

Connections to learning areas such as science and mathematics, physical development, social-emotional development, art, language arts, and social studies can be found in *The Block Book* (Hirsch 1996). The book provides concrete ways of using blocks in the classroom for exploration and learning. "The pleasure of blocks stems primarily from the aesthetic experience," states Hirsch. "It involves the whole person—muscles and senses, intellect and emotion, individual growth and social interaction. Learning results from the imaginative activity, from the need to pose and solve problems" (Hirsch 1996, vii). At Sarah Ward Preschool in Newark, a young child began building a cathedral during free block play. This led to much classroom discussion about a cathedral near the school and its striking appearance (especially at night). It resulted in a school trip to the cathedral.

Through extended discussions and natural curriculum links like these, wood block creations gain complexity in design and richness in meaning.

Steps of the process

The steps that follow guide teachers through the wood sculpture process. They are designed for use over several days or weeks (Samaras & Freer 2003).

1. Order wood scraps (see "Suppliers") or ask local lumberyards or home building stores for scraps. The children can collect twigs, small branches, nuts, acorns, leaves, and other natural resources. Bases for the sculptures can be purchased or made from cut-up corrugated cardboard boxes or larger scraps of wood. They need to be strong enough to hold a heavy block structure. A good size for a base is about 12 inches by 12 inches.

2. Identify books about building, sculpture, architecture, or wood to encourage discussion, vocabulary building, and exploration. Books for adults with pictures of interesting buildings or sculptures help children focus on specific elements of design. Introduce the books to the class and then make them available in the wood center (see #3) for children to look at. Read aloud children's books that address construction, change, or creativity (see "Children's Books Related to Wood Sculpture"). Discuss them with small groups of children to help them make sense of what they have seen and read. If they ask questions you cannot answer, work with them to find the answers, showing them that you are a learner as well.

3. Create a wood center. Leave the wood for sculptures loose in a bin for children to explore. Play and discovery are critical in yielding imaginative results later. During their wood explorations, children will use the ideas they have gotten from the books. Allow several days or weeks for this stage.

4. Put the sculpture bases in the wood center and suggest that children play with the loose wood

Just Enough Glue

Triada uses a rhyme to help children learn how to get just enough glue on a Popsicle stick, and then onto their wood pieces: "Tap, tap, tap, / Wipe, wipe, wipe, / Spread, spread, spread / Like jelly on the bread."

"Tap, tap, tap" is for tapping the Popsicle stick on the side of the container to get rid of some excess glue; "Wipe, wipe, wipe" reminds children to wipe the Popsicle stick on the side of the container to get rid of more excess; and "Spread, spread, spread" tells children to spread the glue onto the wood piece to be attached.

pieces on a base. Join the children in the center. Talk about arranging the wood in various configurations and then making changes. Talk about balance, shapes, sizes, and textures of the wood pieces. Include new vocabulary in your discussions.

5. Introduce wood glue, distributed in deli containers and applied with Popsicle sticks or tongue depressors. Show the whole class how to use the glue. (Do not show the children how to build sculptures, since this may limit their creativity.) Explain how glue is used to attach wood pieces permanently to each other and to the base. Emphasize the importance of experimenting to see where a piece of wood best fits before gluing it.

Make a few mistakes when you demonstrate techniques: glue large pieces with too little glue and note that the piece will not stick. Glue small pieces with huge amounts of glue and note that the glue and the wood pieces slide or that the wood scrap drowns in the glue. Ask the children if you're doing things correctly and how you might do them better. Children love to help out on this. They learn to experiment if something doesn't work the first time. Talk to children about how difficult you find gluing, so they know that it's normal to get a bit frustrated, and so they will feel competent when they are able to do it themselves.

Now the children are ready to make their sculptures.

6. Have children glue larger wood pieces to the base first. Work with small groups in the wood center so you can provide help when children need it. Ask children questions about their work:

- How will adding this piece change the sculpture?
- When you look at your sculpture, what do you see?
- Is this sculpture made mostly of flat pieces or round pieces?

7. Continue the project for days or even weeks so children can add pieces to their sculptures. Encourage them to use a variety of shapes, sizes, and colors. Be sure children turn their bases around to look at their sculpture from different vantage points. This may give them new ideas about where to add pieces of wood and new perspectives on their work. Consider having the children paint and add collage items (fabric, paper, ribbon, string, pom-poms, feathers, beads) to their sculptures.

Continue discussing children's work with them. Introduce the concept *three-dimensional* in a discussion, explaining that sculpture is a three-dimensional art form. Introduce older children to the concept of positive and negative space. A teacher might explain that positive space is the wood and negative space is the air around the wood.

Children's Books Related to Wood Sculpture

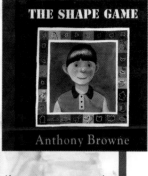

Barton, B. 1990. *Building a house.* New York: Harper Trophy.

Browne, A. 2003. *The shape game.* New York: Farrar Straus Giroux.

Fleming, D. 1996. *Where once there was a wood.* New York: Henry Holt.

Hoban, T. 1983. *Round and round and round.* New York: William Morrow.

Hoban, T. 1986. *Shapes, shapes, shapes.* New York: William Morrow.

Hunter, R.A. 1998. *Cross a bridge.* New York: Holiday House.

Hutchins, P. 1971. *Changes, changes.* New York: Aladdin.

Johnson, A. 2001. *Those building men.* New York: Blue Sky Press.

Jonas, A. 1983. *Round-trip.* New York: Scholastic.

Katz, K. 1999. *The colors of us.* New York: Henry Holt.

Laden, N. 2000. *Roberto the insect architect.* San Francisco: Chronicle Books.

Lipman, J. 1980. *Calder's universe.* New York: Viking. (For adults as well. There are many photos of Calder's sculptures that young children find enjoyable.)

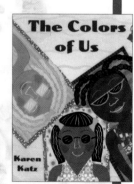

Pinkwater, D.M. 1977. *The big orange splot.* New York: Scholastic.

Udry, J.M. 1987. *A tree is nice.* New York: Harper Trophy.

Yenawine, P. 1991. *Shapes.* New York: Delacorte Press.

8. Hold a group discussion about the finished sculptures, encouraging individual children to share their work with their classmates. Ask children about the process of creating the sculpture as well as the finished product. Discuss with families how to talk to their children about art (more on this below). Explain the benefits children gain from participating in the project. Have the children host a sculpture exhibition in their classroom. This makes a wonderful forum for family-school activity. Children can act as museum tour guides for the visitors—and for children from other classes.

Using language appropriately

Working with Triada, teachers in the Creative Beginnings program learn how to talk to children about the art-making process to maximize learning and the development of higher-order thinking skills such as analysis, synthesis, and evaluation (Bloom 1956). According to Judith Burton,

> Teaching through dialogue is not a laissez-faire pedagogical practice, nor a free-for-all conversation. For dialogue to promote learning, it needs to be thoughtfully structured around a sequence of questions that invite reflection. Sometimes a dialogue may be structured with specific learning in mind and at other times leading toward exploration and discovery. However, it always presupposes that the teacher knows enough about children's perceptions to pace the interchange to their needs, capacities, interests, and levels of understanding. (2000, 330)

In professional development sessions with teachers, Triada emphasizes the power of language used in all phases of the art-making process, from introduction of materials through closure of the activity: "The words used by the teachers can hamper or enhance the

"Tell Me about This"

Begin a dialogue with a child by urging gently, "Tell me about this." Take dictation from younger children. Write their explanations about their sculptures on sticky notes and attach them to the sculptures. (Some children will be able to write these notes themselves.) When a child sees that the teacher has documented the discussion on a sticky note, he or she is affirmed as an artist and a communicator.

success of the visual art process, as words have the tremendous power to awaken the child to imagination, observation, investigation, exploration, planning, utilization, contemplation, and reflection with the art materials." The language used in this process falls into three categories: questions, vocabulary, and concepts.

Questions

Triada asks open-ended questions that require children to think about their creations and why they made particular choices. Here are some introductory questions to use early in the project, when children are first exploring wood pieces in the block center:

• Which block did you choose? Why?

• Where did that block come from?

• How many ways can you place the block so that it will stand up?

• How can you make it higher in space?

These questions require children to analyze, synthesize, and evaluate.

It is important to avoid questions that do not facilitate the art-making process. Never begin with a "naming" question, such as "What is it?" or even worse, "Is that a car?" Questions like these limit the child's range of answers and may interrupt the art-making process because the child feels pressured to come up with a single word to describe a complex creation. Especially avoid declarative statements like "It's a bird!" because the sculpture may have nothing to do with the child's concept of "bird."

The question "What is it?" can intimidate a child who has just built a block creation. It may elicit one-word answers—"A boat" or "A car" or "I don't know"—if any. Furthermore, merely naming an object requires less reflection than explaining how or why it was created. A good question is, "Can you tell me about how you made this?" or "What were you thinking about as you worked today?"

Art Evolves

As children add pieces of wood to their sculptures, they may come up with new ideas, especially after some time has passed. A child's sculpture may start out as a vehicle that later changes to a creature and ends up a robot. Talk about making changes to what has already been done. Welcome such changes as evidence of the creative process. Talk to the children about what it means to be "finished" when they tell you they are done.

Change during the art-making process is similar to the revision/editing phase of the writing process. If the children have experienced the writing process, you can stress this link.

For example, a small group of four- and five-year-olds at Bethany Academy worked together in the wood center using the largest, sturdiest blocks to create a wood sculpture of the White House. When Triada asked them to talk about their work, they explained that they used strong blocks because "the White House can't move a muscle. When you shake the table, it won't move or fall. When you blow it, it can't fall." The children continued, "The president lives there, George Bush. A lot of dollars live there too, maybe $120. It has a beach. George Bush makes copies of dollars with a machine in the White House. The White House also has a drum. George Bush plays the drum with his children."

Teachers' questions can lead to rich and thoughtful discussions that enhance children's thinking and promote learning. While children are creating their sculptures, teachers can help them consider their wood choices when they ask,

- Tell me about what you are doing.
- What made you think of using wood that way?
- Did you see anyone else at your table using wood the same way?
- Would you explain to your neighbor how you built that?

Triada emphasizes that teachers' asking children about their sculptures guides children in their dialogues with each other about their artwork. She often uses circle time to engage in this kind of communication. When a child shows his or her sculpture at circle time, Triada asks the child to tell the class about the piece. She then encourages other children to ask questions about it. For instance, Triada may begin by saying, "I notice that you used a lot of round pieces." She then asks other children to share what they notice about the sculpture.

Triada walks around the room and encourages children to talk to each other when they are working. She asks them to tell their neighbor about what they are doing or to notice what their neighbor is doing. Children soon catch on to how to talk to each other about their work. Verbalizing their ideas and explaining how they accomplished specific tasks substantially enriches the learning process for children.

Burton writes that "the virtues of teaching through dialogue in the arts are many . . . [I]t inhibits the kind of uniformity of outcome in making and appraising that is the consequence of 'telling and demonstration'"(2000, 330).

Vocabulary

Vocabulary building is woven into the art-making and questioning processes. Teachers can ask questions that build vocabulary, such as,

- Are the edges of this piece *smooth* or *rough*?
- Did you use more pieces with *straight* edges or with *round* edges?

Teachers' questions can lead to rich and thoughtful discussions that enhance children's thinking and promote learning.

Wood Word Wall

Here are the contents of a word wall (see Houle & Krogness 2001) compiled by the children:

wood, branch, limb, tree, pine, maple, oak, birch, sawdust, driftwood, knot, plank, rectangle, square, circle, tall, small, short, fat, thin, narrow, wide, artist, sculptor, carpenter, architect, termite, ant, leaf, bud, root, light, dark, saw, hammer, nail, glue, wood glue, dowel, furniture, sculpture, paper, seasons of the tree (spring/summer/fall/winter), berry, change, sandpaper, shellac, wood scrap, base, attach, connect, fix, build, construct, sculpt, deciduous, evergreen, lumber, chain saw, log cabin.

• What shape is this piece that you put *beside/behind/under/on top of/next to/near* the *rectangle*?

Introducing vocabulary words while giving instructions and reinforcing them while asking questions helps children learn new words in a meaningful context. It is a good way for children to learn about shapes because they can handle and examine a shape while learning its name. Introduce words like *rough, smooth, curved, straight, round, flat, edge, line, behind, beside, above, below, under, over, near.*

Teachers can use words posted on a wall in the classroom in dialogues with children during sculpture time or in contexts other than art making. Look for new words in children's books related to the sculpture unit (see "Children's Books Related to Wood Sculpture"). Words from the wall can be sent home for parents to use with their children and suggested for use during writing time both at home and in class.

Concepts

Teachers have a great deal of influence over children's developing creativity and the dynamic in the classroom. This influence is evident in an examination of the concepts or "slogans" Triada uses with young children.

When introducing the wood blocks, shapes, and pieces to the children, Triada takes time to experiment in front of the whole class, and she talks to them about her "failures." She stacks different shapes from the wood bin and says, "Now, what will happen if . . . I pile them up like this . . . and . . . Yikes! They all fell down!" Children seem to especially love this demonstration. They watch intently, seeing that it is okay for a teacher

to "mess up." Triada says to the children, "Do I cry? No! I try, try, try again!" It is vital for children to understand that in making art, there are no mistakes.

Often, what seem like failures when making art can lead to new and better creative solutions and even more learning opportunities for the children. Triada asks, "Can we think of another way to make this work?" She explains that this is the way artists create—with a lot of imagination, patience, and hard work. Teachers can help children apply this concept to other areas of the classroom and to the larger world.

Conclusion

Burton states,

A good dialogue will allow an interweaving of personal sensory, affective, and cognitive responses as youngsters reflect on their experiences and, through imaginative reconstruction, give them voice in and through visual materials. It will promote self-reflection, recognition, and tolerance for diversity, and an ability to listen to and learn from the thoughts of others. In addition, a thoughtful dialogue will offer youngsters insights into how ideas are constructed, relate to each other in sequence, and build in complexity to larger ideas. It gives meaning to an individual's personal development by opening them to the powers of scrutiny, investigation, inquiry, and questioning by others. (2000, 330)

At Sarah Ward Preschool, a young artist explained to Triada, "Last week, I made this sculpture and I only used a few blocks. That's because I was only still little then. Now I am big, and I am using many more blocks, and I can double stack them to build a very tall tower. Look! I don't cry! I try, try, try again!"

References

Bloom, B.S. 1956. *Taxonomy of educational objectives: The classification of educational goals: Handbook I, cognitive domain.* Available online: http://faculty.washington.edu/krumme/guides/bloom.html.

Burton, J. 2000. The configuration of meaning: Learner-centered art education revisited. *Studies in Art Education* 41 (4): 330–42.

Edwards, C., L. Gandini, & G. Forman. 1998. *The hundred languages of children: The Reggio Emilia approach, advanced reflections.* Rev. ed. Greenwich, CT: Ablex.

Hirsch, E. S., ed. 1996. *The block book.* 3rd ed. Washington, DC: NAEYC.

Houle, A., & A. Krogness. 2001. The wonders of word walls. *Young Children* 56 (5): 92–93.

Samaras, T., & P.K. Freer. 2003. Sculpture and words: Constructing understanding. Presentation at the National Art Education Association Conference, April, in Minneapolis.

For more information about the Creative Beginnings program, contact Corinna Bisgaier at cbisgaier@yanj.org or visit the Young Audiences of New Jersey Web site at www.yanj.org.

Books for Young Children
about the Creative Arts

Compiled by Sandi Collins

About painters and other artists

The Art Lesson. T. dePaola. 1997. Puffin reprint. An autobiographical exercise for the child with a single-minded interest or special talent. Ages 4–8.

The Art of Eric Carle. E. Carle. 2002. Philomel. A journey into the creative mind of a children's book illustrator. Ages 4–8.

A Bird or 2: A Story about Henri Matisse. B. Le Tord. 1999. Eerdmans. Depicts Matisse painting with bright, bold colors. Ages 4–8.

Camille and The Sunflowers: A Story about Vincent Van Gogh. L. Anholt. 1994. Barrons Juveniles. A young boy and his family befriend a lonely stranger and admire his unusual paintings. Based on true story. Ages 4–8.

A Child's Book of Art: Great Pictures, First Words. L. Micklethwait. 1993. DK Publishing. Themes place

Sandi Collins is associate production coordinator for *Young Children*.

Note: Older books on this list may be unavailable at your local library, but can be obtained through Internet book distributors.

artworks in contexts familiar to children (family, pets, colors, opposites, work, and play). Simple words and short phrases accompany each painting. Ages 4–8.

David's Drawings. C. Falwell. 2001. Lee & Low. A shy African American boy makes friends with his classmates by drawing a picture of a tree. Ages 4–8.

DaVinci. M. Venezia. 1989. (Getting to Know the World's Greatest Artists series.) Children's Press. Traces the life of the artist whose knowledge of nature made his paintings seem alive. Ages 4–8.

Diego Rivera (Life and Work of . . .). A.R. Schaefer. 2003. Heinemann. A look at the life and work of the twentieth-century Mexican painter. Ages 4–8.

Dinner at Magritte's. M. Garland. 1995. Dutton. A young boy escapes from boredom to the neighbors' house where he is introduced to the worlds of Salvador Dali and other surrealist artists. Ages 4–8.

The Dot. P.H. Reynolds. 2003. Candlewick. When the teacher tells a reluctant artist to "just make a mark," the girl sets off on a journey of discovery, self-expression, and growth. Ages 4–8.

Dreaming Pictures. J. von Schemm. 1997. Children's Book Press. (Adventures in Art series.) Prestel. Explores the paintings of artist Paul Klee (1879–1940) and his dream world. Ages 4–8.

Family Pictures/Cuadros de familia. C. Lomas Garza. 1990. A series of paintings of the author's childhood in Texas near the Mexican border is narrated in English and Spanish. Ages 4–8.

Frida. J. Winter. Illus., A. Juan. 2002. Arthur A. Levine Books/Scholastic Press. An exploration of the work of twentieth century artist Frida Kahlo. Ages 4–8.

Frida Kahlo: The Artist Who Painted Herself. M. Frith. Illus., T. dePaolo. 2003. Grosset & Dunlap. An introduction to the avant-garde Mexican painter, told from the viewpoint of a girl doing a report. Ages 4–8.

Grandma Moses (Life and Work of . . .). A.R. Schaefer. 2003. Heinemann. Examines the life and work of the twentieth-century American folk painter. Ages 4–8.

Hands: Growing Up to Be an Artist. L. Ehlert. 2004. Harcourt. All an artist needs is a special place to work, supplies and tools, and lots of encouragement to nurture the creative spirit. Ages 4–8.

Harold and the Purple Crayon. C. Johnson. 1981. 50th anniversary ed. HarperCollins. A small boy goes for a walk—crayon in hand—and draws himself some wonderful adventures. Ages 4–8.

Harriet and the Promised Land. J. Lawrence. 1997. Aladdin reprint. This tribute to Harriet Tubman introduces the work of African American artist Jacob Lawrence (1917–2000). Ages 4–8.

Henri Matisse: Drawing with Scissors. J. O'Connor. Illus., J. Hartland. 2002. (Smart about Art series.) Grosset & Dunlap. Done in the style of a grade-school report, the book covers the Fauve movement and Matisse's shift from painting to cut-paper collage. Ages 4–8.

I Can Draw a Weeposaur and Other Dinosaurs. E. Greenfield. Illus., J.S. Gilchrist. 2001. Greenwillow. Poems depict a young girl drawing the sleeposaurus and other imaginary dinosaurs. Ages 4–8.

Ish. P.H. Reynolds. 2004. Candlewick. When his older brother makes fun of his drawing, Ramon is crushed until he discovers that his sister has been saving his work and that creativity is not exactitude. Ages 4–8.

I Spy an Alphabet in Art. L. Micklethwait. 1992. Greenwillow. Readers interact with 26 classic paintings that pair the I Spy game with the timeless works of art. Ages 4–8.

I Spy Shapes in Art. L. Micklethwait. 2004. Greenwillow. Pairs the classic game of I Spy with timeless art to challenge readers to look closely. Ages 4–8.

In the Garden with Van Gogh. J. Merberg. Illus., S. Bober. 2002. Chronicle. Van Gogh's sleepy trees, golden haystacks, and juicy fruits are paired with playful rhyming text. Ages infant–preschool.

Katie and the Mona Lisa. J. Mayhew. 1999. Orchard. At the art museum, Katie steps into the famous painting where she and Mona Lisa meet characters from four other well-known Renaissance paintings. Ages 4–8.

Katie and The Sunflowers. J. Mayhew. 2001. Orchard. Katie steps in and out of five paintings by Van Gogh, Gauguin, and Cezanne. Ages 4–8.

Katie Meets the Impressionists. J. Mayhew. 1999. Orchard. Katie climbs into five impressionist paintings. Ages 4–8.

Landscapes. C. Delafosse. Illus., T. Ross. 1996. (First Discovery Art series.) Scholastic. Die-cut pages, interactive transparent overlays, and factual text help introduce the paintings of landscape masters. Ages 4–8.

The Legend of the Indian Paintbrush. T. dePaola. 1996. Puffin reprint. The tale of how the Indian paintbrush, the state flower of Wyoming, first bloomed and how a young Indian dreamed of creating a painting that captures the beauty of a sunset. Ages 4–8.

Liang and the Magic Paintbrush. Demi. 1988. Henry Holt. A Chinese folktale in which a beggar boy's wit and art help him thwart a greedy emperor's plan. Ages 4–8.

Lunchtime for a Purple Snake. H. Zieffert. Illus., T. McKie. 2003. Houghton Mifflin. A patient artist teaches his granddaughter to paint. Preschool.

A Magical Day with Matisse. J. Merberg. Illus., S. Bober. 2002. Chronicle. Music, color, bobbing sailboats, tickled toes, and rhyming text. Ages infant–preschool.

Marianthe's Story: Painted Words and **Marianthe's Story: Spoken Memories.** Aliki. 1998. Greenwillow. Two stories based on the author/illustrator's childhood experiences. Although Mari starts school knowing no one and unable to speak or understand the language, she expresses herself and her feelings through art. Ages 4–8.

Mary Cassatt: Family Pictures. J. O'Connor. Illus., J. Kalis. 2003. (Smart about Art series.) Grosset & Dunlap. The life and the work of the American Impressionist painter, as told from a child's point of view. Ages 4–8.

Masterpiece of the Month. J. Thomas. Illus., B. Apodaca and T. Wright. 1998. Teacher Created Materials. Explores artistic concepts through great works of art and follow-up activities.

Michelangelo. M. Venezia. 1992. (Getting to Know the World's Greatest Artists series.) Children's Press. Describes the life and art of the Italian Renaissance painter/sculptor. Ages 4–8.

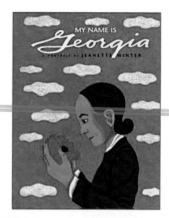

My Name Is Georgia: A Portrait by Jeanette Winter. J. Winter. 1998. Silver Whistle. Evokes the uniqueness of American painter Georgia O'Keeffe, starting with her views of the world as a child and following her dreams throughout life. Ages 4–8.

No Good in Art. 1980. M. Cohen. Illus., L. Hoban. Greenwillow. A first-grader is convinced he can't draw, but when encouraged, demonstrates he can. Ages 4–8.

No One Saw: Ordinary Things Through the Eyes of an Artist. B. Raczka. 2001. Millbrook. Looks at individual modern painters and the special way in which we all see the world. Ages 4–8.

Paintings. C. Delafosse. Illus., T. Ross. 1996. (First Discovery Art series.) Scholastic. Presents famous paintings from around the world using die-cut and transparent pages. Ages 4–8.

Picasso and the Girl with a Ponytail: A Story about Pablo Picasso. L. Anholt. 1998. Barrons Juveniles. Shy Sylvette gradually begins to gain self-confidence during the summer she models for the renowned artist. Ages 4–8.

A Picnic with Monet. J. Merberg. Illus., S. Bober. 2003. Chronicle. Claude Monet's light-filled paintings take children on a picnic in the countryside. Ages infant–preschool.

Pictures for Miss Josie. S. Belton. Illus., B. Andrews. 2003. The story of Josephine Carroll Smith (Miss Josie) and a young artist who became one of her friends. Ages 4–8.

Portraits. C. Delafosse. Illus., T. Ross. 1995. (First Discovery Art series.) Scholastic. Introduces famous portraits through interactive overlays and die-cut pages. Ages 4–8.

Setting the Turkeys Free. W. Nikola-Lisa . Illus., K. Wilson-Max. 2004. Hyperion. A boy makes traditional handprint turkeys but lets his imagination—and the birds—soar. Preschool.

The Starry Night. N. Waldman. 1999. Boyds Mills. A boy and Vincent Van Gogh embark on a tour of the museum. When the artist's painting disappears, the boy is inspired to create his own copy of it. Ages 4–8.

Vincent Van Gogh: Sunflowers and Swirly Stars. J. Holub. Illus., B. Bucks. 2001. (Smart about Art series.) Grossett & Dunlap. Explores the ups and downs of Van Gogh's life and art, pairing funny cartoons with reproductions of classic paintings. Ages 4–8.

What Is an Artist? B. Lehn. Photog., C. Krauss. 2002. Millbrook. Ages 4–7. Explains what artists do and shows children engaged in those activities.

When Pigasso Met Mootisse. N. Laden. 1998. Chronicle. When conflicts arise, a talented pig and his artistic bull neighbor build fences that ultimately become modern art masterpieces. Includes biographies of real-life artists Henri Matisse and Pablo Picasso. Ages 4–8.

Willy's Pictures. A. Browne. 2000. Candlewick. Willy the chimp paints pictures that are tributes to art masterpieces. Ages 4–8.

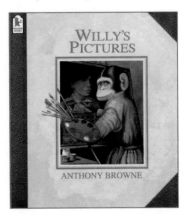

The Year with Grandma Moses. W. Nikola-Lisa. and G. Moses. 2000. Henry Holt. A collection of paintings and memoirs by the folk artist describing the seasons and related activities in rural upstate New York. Ages 4–8.

Music

Ah, Music! Aliki. 2003. HarperCollins. Aliki shares her insight about music and its themes and variations. Ages 5 and up.

Aïda. L. Price. Illus., L. & D. Dillon. 1990. Harcourt Brace Jovanovich. Leontyne Price retells the famous opera about the beautiful princess of Ethiopia. Ages 4–8.

Animal Orchestra. I. Orleans. Illus., T. Gergely. 2001. Golden Books reprint. A rhyming story about an animal orchestra and its hippo conductor. Ages infant–preschool.

Carnival of the Animals: Classical Music for Kids (with CD). C. Saint-Saens, with B.C. Turner. Illus., S. Williams. 1999. Henry Holt. A musical joke by composer Camille Saint-Saëns, the *Carnival of the Animals.* introduces classical music through whimsical illustration, text, and melodies. Ages 4–8.

Charlie Parker Played Be Bop. C. Raschka. 1992. Orchard. A picture book about legendary jazzman Charlie Parker (1920–1955) and his cat. Ages 4–8.

Hip Cat. J. London. Illus., W. Hubbard. 1996. Chronicle. A naive saxophone-playing cat journeys to San Francisco to live his dream of being a jazz musician. Ages 4–8.

The Jazz Fly (with CD). M. Gollub. Illus., K. Hanke. 2000. Tortuga. While seeking directions to town, a fly picks up the rhythm of the answers he gets from a frog, a hog, a donkey,

and a dog and then uses the sounds to jazz up his band's music. Ages 4–8.

John Coltrane's Giant Steps. C. Raschka. 2002. Atheneum. A visual deconstruction of the jazz saxophonist's composition. Ages 4–8.

M Is for Music. K. Krull. Illus., S. Innerst. Harcourt. Playful text introduces the world of music. Ages 4–8.

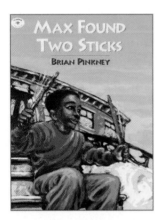

Max Found Two Sticks. B. Pinkney. 1997. Aladdin. Max doesn't feel like talking, but he responds to questions by drumming on various objects, including a bucket, hat boxes, and garbage cans, echoing the city sounds around him. Ages 4–8.

Meet the Orchestra. A. Hayes. Illus., K. Thompson. 1995. Voyager. Poetic descriptions and illustrations portray the sounds and imagery of the orchestra. Ages 4–8.

Music, Music for Everyone. B.B. Williams. 1992. Greenwillow. Rosa plays her accordion with her friends in the Oak Street Band and earns money to help with expenses while her grandmother is sick. Ages 4–8.

Musical Instruments from A to Z. B. Kalman. 1997. (AlphaBasiCs series.) Crabtree. A broad assortment of instruments and their history are introduced through a question-and-answer format. Ages 4–8.

My Family Plays Music. J. Cox. Illus., E. Brown. 2003. Holiday House. A picture book that explores 10 different types of music through the eyes and ears of a young African American. Ages 4–8.

Perfect Harmony: A Musical Journey with the Boys Choir of Harlem. C.R. Smith Jr. 2002. Hyperion. Playful poems for musical inspiration. Ages 4–8.

Shake, Rattle, and Roll: The Founders of Rock and Roll. H. George-Warren. Illus., L. Levine. 2004. Sandpiper. Ages 4–8. Presents illustrations and descriptions of early rock-and-rollers, such as Bill Haley and Buddy Holly.

The Story of the Incredible Orchestra: An Introduction to Musical Instruments and the Symphony Orchestra. B. Koscielniak. 2000. Houghton Mifflin. A look at the history of the orchestra and its instruments. Ages 4–8.

A Tisket, A Tasket. E. Fitzgerald. Illus., O. Eitan. 2003. Philomel. A picture book rendition of Ella Fitzgerald's (1917–1996) musical reworking of the nursery song. Ages 4–8.

What Instrument Is This? R. Hausherr. 1992. Scholastic. Ages 3–8. Photos introduce children to 18 instruments of the orchestra.

When Marian Sang: True Recital of Marian Anderson. P.M. Ryan. Illus., B. Selznick. 2002. Scholastic. A tribute to the gifted singer who broke racial barriers to become a world-renowned performer. Ages 4–8.

Woody Guthrie: Poet of the People. B. Christensen. 2001. Knopf. A biography of folk legend Woody Guthrie and a social history of the challenging times he lived in. Ages 4–8.

Zin! Zin! Zin! A Violin. L. Moss. Illus., M. Priceman. 1995. Simon & Schuster. A counting book that introduces the orchestra through rhyme and artwork. Ages 4–8.

Sculpture/Architecture

Alexander Calder (Life and Work of...). A.R. Schaefer. 2003. Heinemann. Examines the life and work of the twentieth-century American sculptor. Ages 4–8.

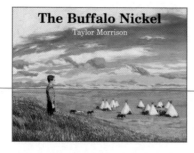

The Buffalo Nickel. T. Morrison. 2002. Houghton Mifflin. Depicts the history and making of the buffalo nickel through the story of its creator, American sculptor James Fraser. Ages 4–8.

Dream Carver. D. Cohn. Illus., A. Cordova. 2002. Chronicle. Tells of Mateo, a young woodcarver who

bravely breaks with a generations-old artistic tradition. Inspired by the life of Oaxacan carver Manual Jimenez. Ages 4–8.

Gugu's House. C. Stock. 2001. Clarion. Ages 5–8. In Zimbabwe, Kukamba visits her grandmother, Gugu, who paints and creates clay sculptures. When the art pieces are destroyed by long-awaited rains, Gugu shows her granddaughter the beauty that nature has created.

Henry Moore: From Bones and Stones to Sketches and Sculptures. J.M. Gardner. 1993. Simon & Schuster. An exploration of the British sculptor's creative process as he progresses from sketch to model to monument. Ages 4–8.

Maya Lin. A. Stone. 2003. Raintree. Presents the life of the young architect-sculptor who designed the Vietnam War Memorial. Ages 4–8.

The Wonderful Towers of Watts. P. Zelver. Illus., F. Lessac. 1994. William Morrow. Describes how Simon Rodia, an Italian immigrant with no art or architectural training, created three tower masterpieces in his inner-city Los Angeles backyard. Ages 4–8.

Dance

Baby Dance. A. Taylor. Illus., M. van Heerden. 1999. HarperFestival. A playful poem with father and child dancing across the pages. Ages infant–preschool.

Baby Danced the Polka. K. Beaumont. Illus., J. Plecas. 2004. Dial. Ages 4–8. In this colorful flap book, each time the baby is put down for a nap, no sleep takes place. Instead, the baby dances with the partners found under each flap.

Barnyard Dance. B. Boynton. 1993. Workman. Singing and dancing farm animals. Ages infant–preschool.

Dance Me a Story: Twelve Tales from the Classic Ballets. J. Rosenberg. 1993. Hudson. Retells 12 ballets as fairy tales. Ages 4–8.

Dancing with Degas. J. Merberg. Illus., S. Bober. 2003. Chronicle. Toe shoes, tutus, and elegant ballerinas shown in the works of Edward Degas. Ages infant–preschool.

Giraffes Can't Dance. G. Andreae., Illus., G. Parker-Rees. 2002. Orchard. A rhyming tale of inclusion for those who march to the beat of a different cricket. Ages infant–preschool.

The Little Ballerina. H.L. Ross. 1996. Random House. A dancer practices the five basic positions, works at the barre, and struggles to do a perfect pirouette while preparing for a recital performance. Ages 4–8.

Maria Tallchief, Prima Ballerina. V. Browne. 1995. Modern. Tells the story of the Native American who danced to fame with the New York City Ballet. Ages 4–8.

My Mama Had a Dancing Heart. L.M. Gray. Illus., R. Colon. 1996. Orchard. Recounts the memories of a ballet dancer whose mother celebrated the wonders of the natural world through dance. Ages infant–preschool.

On Your Toes: A Ballet ABC. R. Isadora. 2003. Greenwillow. A diverse group of girls and boys prance and pose through the alphabet, demonstrating the grace, drama, and dedication required for ballet. Ages 4–8.

Rap A Tap Tap: Here's Bojangles—Think of That! L. Dillon. and D. Dillon. 2002. Blue Sky Press. A tribute, in the style of Harlem Renaissance artist Aaron Douglas, to African American tap dancer Bill "Bojangles" Robinson (1878-1949), who "danced in the street" and "made art with his feet." Ages 4–8.

Drama/Theater

All the World's a Stage. R.P. Davidson. Illus. A. Lobel. 2003. Greenwillow. Applauds inspiration, creation, story, and the world and works of William Shakespeare. Ages 4–8.

Drama School. M. Manning. Illus., B. Granstrom. 1999. Larousse Kingfisher Chambers. Write a script, learn to act, build a stage set, shoot a movie. An introduction to the basics of theater and film. Ages 4–8.

Mouse Theater. M. Cartlidge. 1992. Dutton. A lift-the-flap book follows a troupe of theater mice staging plays from town to town. Ages infant–preschool.

Theater Magic: Behind the Scenes at a Children's Theater. C.W. Bellville. 1986. Carolrhoda. Photographic essay on an adaptation of Hans Christian Andersen's "The Nightingale," describing how the play is planned, designed, cast, and rehearsed. Ages 4–8.

The Year I Didn't Go To School. G. Potter. 2002. Atheneum. The author tells of touring Italy, at the age of seven, with her family's tiny theater company. Ages 4–8

Textiles

Luka's Quilt. G. Guback. 1994. Greenwillow. Grandma Tutu is hurt when Luka is disappointed with the traditional Hawaiian quilt Tutu made for her. All ends well though. Ages 4–8.

Pieces: A Year in Poems and Quilts. A.G. Hines. 2001. Greenwillow. Nineteen handmade designs are paired with an original poem about the seasons of the year. Ages 4–8.

Photography

All Around Town: The Photographs of Richard Samuel Roberts. D. Johnson. 1998. Henry Holt. The pride, joy, and strength of a bustling community reflected in the photographs of an African American artist Ages 4–up.

Click! A Book about Cameras and Taking Pictures. G. Gibbons. 1997. Little Brown. Introduction to the art of photography. Ages 4–8.

My First Photography Book. D. King. 1994. DK Publishing. Advice to help young children take exciting photographs with a simple fixed focus or disposable camera. Suggested at-home projects using developed prints. Ages 4–8.

Poetry

Bow Wow Meow Meow. D. Florian. Twenty-one poems about favorite animal friends. Ages 4–8.

A Box of Animal Crackers. J. Dyer. A set of three board books filled with pictures, poems, and lullabies. Ages 9 months–3.

Chicka Chicka Boom Boom. B. Martin Jr., John Archambault. 1991. Little Simon. Ages 4–8. This is a rhythmic alphabet book in which the letters agree to meet each other at the top of a coconut tree. The weight is too much for the tree and the letters come tumbling down.

Frederick. L. Lionni. 1967. Knopf. A day-dreaming poet mouse stores up something special for the long cold winter. Ages 4–8.

Hand Rhymes. M. Brown. Finger plays and rhymes in the tradition of Itsy Bitsy Spider. Ages infant–5.

Splish Splash. J.B. Graham. Illus., S.M. Scott. 2001. Houghton Mifflin. Pool poetry. Ages 4–8.

The Sweet and Sour Animal Book. L. Hughes. Illus., Harlem School of the Arts. 1997. Oxford University Press. Langston Hughes portrays the alphabet and the animal world with 26 new poems. Ages 4–8.

Touch the Poem. A. Adoff. Illus., L. Desimini. 2000. Blue Sky Press. Poems and paintings that reflect on the five senses. Ages 4–8.

Visiting Langston. W. Perdomo. Illus., B. Collier. 2002. Henry Holt. A rhythmic tale of a visit by a budding young poet and her father to the Harlem house where poet Langston Hughes (1902-1967) lived. Ages 4–8.

Pottery

Children of Clay: A Family of Pueblo Potters. R. Swentzell. Photo., B. Steen. 1993. First Avenue. Tells of an Indian family in Santa Clara Pueblo, New Mexico, who follow the ages-old pottery traditions of the Tewa people. Ages 7 and up.

The Pot That Juan Built. N. Andrews-Goebel. Illus., D. Diaz. 2002. Lee & Low. Story of Juan Quezada, master Mexican potter who created a folk art community in his small town. Ages 4–8.

When Clay Sings. B. Baylor. Illus., T. Bahti. 1987. Aladdin. Retraces the life of prehistoric southwest Indian tribes in the designs of their pottery. Ages 4–8.

Museums

Art Dog. T. Hurd. 1996. HarperCollins. When the Mona Woofa is stolen from the Dogopolis Museum of Art, a mysterious character tracks down and captures the thieves. Ages 4–8.

Museum ABC. Metropolitian Museum of Art. 2002. Little Brown. An alphabet picture book that introduces more than 100 works of art from the museum's collection. Ages 4–8.

Museum 123. Metropolitan Museum of Art. 2004. Little Brown. 2004. A simple approach to numbers, illustrated from the museum's collection. Ages 4–8.

You Can't Take a Balloon into the Metropolitan Museum. J.P. Weitzman. Illus., R.P. Glasser. 1998. Dial. Chaos ensues when a girl's balloon gets loose in New York City as she and her grandmother visit the museum. Reproductions of famous artworks reflect the balloon's adventures. Ages 4–8.

You Can't Take a Balloon into the Museum of Fine Arts. J.P. Weitzman. Illus., R.P. Glasser. 2002. Dial. A romp through the historical environs of Boston and its renowned museum. Ages 4–8.

You Can't Take a Balloon into the National Gallery. J.P. Weitzman. Illus., R.P. Glasser. 2000. Dial. The famed gallery and majestic monuments of Washington, D.C., provide the setting for a collision of art and urban life. Ages 4–8.

Music Play
Creating Centers for Musical Play and Exploration

Kristen M. Kemple, Jacqueline J. Batey, and Lynn C. Hartle

Music is in the air in Ms. Viola's Head Start classroom. She has a large collection of CDs, most of which were recorded specifically for children. Music often plays in the background during greeting, snack, choice, and nap times.

Music is in use in Mr. Kerry's pre-K classroom. "Piggyback" songs remind children of expected behaviors and add a pleasant dose of calm to transitions that might otherwise become chaotic.

Music is on the lips of Mrs. Rosetti's kindergartners. Morning circle begins with a greeting song, followed by children's selection of two more songs from the class's impressive repertoire. Afternoon circle is the time for learning and practicing new songs.

Each of these teachers might say, "My classroom is very musical," and each is providing something of value.

The presence of music in young children's lives can sometimes be taken for granted. In most early childhood classrooms, teachers and children sing a song or two at circle time. Many teachers use musical strategies to help children handle transitions (for example, singing "We're cleaning up our room, we're cleaning up our room, we're putting all the blocks away, we're cleaning up our room" to the tune of "The Farmer in the Dell"). Parents often sing lullabies and traditional rhymes to their young children. At home and in the car, parents play recorded music they themselves enjoy. They may play a "kid's'" tape or CD to keep the children happy and occupied on the road. Music certainly is present in the lives of many young children.

Nevertheless, there is a growing awareness that music is underused and underaddressed in early childhood education (Kenney 1997). In the early years, musical aptitude is still developing. Infancy and early childhood are prime times to capitalize on children's innate musical spontaneity, and to encourage their natural inclinations to sing, move, and play with sound (Stellacio & McCarthy 1999).

Why does music not receive deeper attention in early childhood education? Teachers may not recognize the full value and potential of providing for children's musical development and may not understand

> **I**nfancy and early childhood are prime times to capitalize on children's **innate musical spontaneity,** and to encourage their **natural inclinations to sing, move, and play with sound.**

Kristen M. Kemple, PhD, is an associate professor of early childhood education at the University of Florida in Gainesville, and is a former preschool teacher. She has taught graduate courses in early childhood art and music for many years.

Jacqueline J. Batey, PhD, is an assistant professor in the Charter School of Education at Berry College in Mount Berry, Georgia, where she teaches undergraduate and graduate education courses. She spent many years teaching regular and special education classes in public and private schools in Florida, North Carolina, and Georgia.

Lynn C. Hartle, PhD, is program coordinator and associate professor at the University of Central Florida in Orlando. She teaches undergraduate and graduate play courses, stressing the value of play for children and adults.

Photos © Ellen B. Senisi. Illustrations by Natalie Klein Cavanagh.

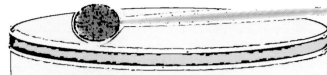

the many ways musical involvement can enhance development and learning in other areas. They may believe that musical development is important only for a small number of highly talented children. They may be intimidated by the specialized expertise of music educators or inhibited by their own lack of knowledge about music education or a perceived lack of musicianship. NAEYC and MENC (National Association of Music Education [formerly the Music Educators National Conference], www. menc.org) are collaborating to promote the full inclusion of music in early childhood curriculum.

> Music permeates the very fiber of Ms. Katie's preschool class. During choice time, she watches and listens as Shira and Maxwell play with a new double set of handbells. The children discover that two of the bells sound exactly alike. She waits to see if they will continue to try to match pitches, then prompts, "I wonder if there are other pairs that sound alike." The two children search for more bells with matching sounds. After finding a second match, the children note with interest that bells that sound alike are also identical in color. Their theory is confirmed when they ring two yellow bells and find them identical in pitch.
>
> Now Ms. Katie steps in with a challenge. She sets up a screen on the table between the two sets of bells and says, "Do you think you can match pitches without seeing the colors?" Maxwell and Shira eagerly respond to her cue and engage in constructive musical play for another 10 minutes.

Ms. Katie intentionally incorporates and facilitates musical development through planned opportunities for play. She also includes plenty of group singing, spontaneous and planned incorporation of music throughout the day, and purposeful integration of a wide variety of high-quality musical recordings of many genres. She appreciates the multifaceted possibilities of music in a developmentally appropriate early childhood program.

Musical play

Young children engage in music as play (Moorhead & Pond 1978; Neely 2001). Though many early childhood educators may not consider themselves musicians or music educators, they generally do feel comfortable with the medium of play.

When offered a variety of drums and strikers, children play with sound. By exploring and "messing

> **Young children engage in music as an exploratory activity, one that is interactive, social, creative, and joyful.**

A Good Early Childhood Music Program Helps Children Learn to . . .

- Sing tunefully
- Move expressively and rhythmically
- Play classroom instruments
- Develop age-appropriate musical concepts
- Create music
- Value music as part of everyday life
- Listen appreciatively
- Develop the following attitudes: I can . . .
  - ♪ listen to music   ♪ play music
  - ♪ understand music   ♪ respond to music with my body
  - ♪ write music   ♪ create music

Source: Isenberg & Jalongo 1993, 109.

around," they discover they can make one sound by striking one drum and a different sound by striking another. Their drum play is supported because adults expect and allow for the "noise."

When young children hear music, they move to it. Supportive adults share their joy and delight in their fun, also listening and moving in response to the music. Once children learn to sing, they create their own melodies and invent their own words to familiar songs. Their song play is supported when adults demonstrate authentic interest, interact with children through song, and engage in their own playful song making.

Play is central to early childhood education (Monighan-Nourot, Scales, & Van Hoorn 1987; Bredekamp & Copple 1997), and it is a primary vehicle for musical growth (Kenney 1997). When early childhood teachers recognize the playful nature of children's musical activity, music education may look more like familiar territory. Young children engage in music as an exploratory activity, one that is interactive, social, creative, and joyful.

Because young children engage in music as play, it makes sense to offer musical activities during choice

time. Most early childhood classrooms have areas for dramatic play, building with blocks, reading books, and creating art. Why not a music center? Providing a center for musical activities is not an idea invented by the authors (see Moomaw 1997 and Andress 1998 for further examples of musical play activities). It is, however, an idea that is seldom implemented in early childhood classrooms. Most preschool programs offer few opportunities for exploring and experimenting with musical sound (Golden 1990; Tarnowski & Barrett 1992). Many of the musical play ideas described in preschool curriculum guides are in fact highly teacher directed and controlled, with narrowly defined expectations and possibilities.

Play is voluntary and intrinsically motivated, whether the motivation is curiosity, affiliation, mastery, or something else. Play is episodic, characterized by emerging and shifting goals that children develop spontaneously and flexibly (Fromberg 1999). Opportunities for musical play are often sacrificed to teacher-controlled activities (Dorman 1990; Tsunady 2001). As a result, the musical experiences offered in early childhood programs can constrain musical creativity because there is too much teacher control and monitoring; children cannot make their own choices about what to do (Rohwer 1997).

Teachers' roles

Teachers do much more to support play than simply allow it to happen. Vygotskian theory describes the role of sociocultural context in child development (Berk & Winsler 1995). From this social-constructivist perspective, children learn through supported interactions with more competent "others"—typically older children or adults. The term *scaffolding* refers to the continuum of supportive structuring that more competent others provide as a child masters a new strategy or skill. As the child internalizes the role of the other and is increasingly able to perform independently, support is gradually withdrawn. This perspective is in contrast to the image of the lone child testing, trying, assimilating, and accommodating in a social vacuum.

From a social-constructivist perspective, adults have to do more than set the stage—for music *or* play—by providing space, time, and materials. There's much more to supporting children's musical development than just pushing the play button on a CD player. When young children have a rich musical environment along with appropriate guidance from adults, they can learn, for example, to imitate and, with increasing precision, distinguish among rhythm and tone patterns (Gordon 1997).

Teachers play multiple roles in supporting children's play activities (Isenberg & Jalongo 1993). They must

plan—set the stage and decide how to introduce new materials in inviting ways.

observe—watch to see how children interact with the materials and each other. Determine if children need help to solve a problem; look for teachable moments.

participate—share and enjoy music and play with children, rather than direct the play or perform for them.

extend—look for the right time to enhance children's exploration by asking a well-chosen—and often open-ended—question, adding a new piece of equipment, or interjecting an idea for consideration.

model—join in and demonstrate a new behavior nonintrusively, via parallel play. When adults model movement to music while also describing their actions and offering suggestions, children engage in more differentiated and synchronized movement (Metz 1989).

motivate—encourage children to take part in the play. This role is particularly important to consider when working with children with certain disabling conditions. Young children with mental retardation, for example, may not spontaneously choose to engage with play materials and need to be motivated through social or even tangible reinforcement to become involved in playful activity (Carta et al. 1991).

When young children have a **rich musical environment** along with **appropriate guidance from adults, they can learn, for example, to imitate and, with increasing precision, distinguish among rhythm and tone patterns.**

Inventing Music Play Centers

"A Good Early Childhood Music Program Helps Children Learn to . . ." (see p. 25) lists general information on developmentally appropriate musical knowledge that can be taught during the early childhood years. When considering the following music play center ideas—offered as examples to stir the reader's imagination—keep in mind the aims and objectives found in this box, as well as the self-directed nature of play and the wide range of ways that teachers may support young children's play.

Using pipe phones

Materials: Purchase segments of PVC pipe at a hardware store, and attach them so they form an arc of the size needed to reach from a child's mouth to her or his ear. Provide the pipe in a listening center with a tape player and recorded music that is easy for young children to sing (simple rhythms, a range of C to G or A, and simple lyrics with repetitive phrases).

Supporting play: The pipe isolates the child's voice, allowing the child to simultaneously listen to the music and hear his or her own voice clearly. This provides opportunities for each child to adjust his singing voice to match or harmonize with the recordings. Pipe phones can be helpful for children with attention deficits or children with hearing impairments.

Have children put one hand on their throat as they sing. This will help them feel the vibration of their vocal chords at the same time their voice is isolated and amplified through the pipe phone.

Creating musical compositions

Materials: Provide a portable keyboard or piano or xylophone/glockenspiel and some paper, markers, and stickers. To the keys corresponding to the middle two octaves, teachers should affix removable stickers of various shapes and sizes, such that each key has a unique sticker.

To simplify, affix stickers only to keys middle C to G. To extend, include more keys. To make a pentatonic scale or five-note scale, put an *x* on the F and B piano keys (or remove the F and B xylophone bars) so children won't play these notes. When two children play instruments adjusted to this scale, anything they play together sounds good.

Supporting play: As children create their own music, encourage them to "write" it down for future reference. They can copy the stickers corresponding to the notes they use, or place identical stickers on a piece of paper. Encourage children to play their own (or their peers') notated music. Children can also invent their own systems of musical notation. For children with limited motor coordination, the striking surface of xylophone bars may be too narrow. Substitute a metallophone, bass xylophone, or single tone bars that can be spread out.

Dancing and movement

Materials: Hang full-length Plexiglas mirrors on a wall or in a corner. Provide a wide variety of music on continuous loop tape to encourage movement and dance—classical waltzes, contemporary, traditional folk dance melodies. Props can help some children feel comfortable and get started dancing. For example, children can use doll partners (large rag dolls with tennis shoes or dish detergent bottle dolls with flowing skirts) or ribbon or crepe paper streamers (attached to cardboard paper towel rolls or shower rings for safety). Observe children's use of props to make sure they are not distracting children from the music and its connection to their movement.

Supporting play: Play along. If children seem stuck, play beside them. Model different movements and describe your actions. To get into the swing, children can view short video clips of various kinds of dancing, such as Irish step dancing (like "Riverdance"), ballet, jazz, or tango. Provide the opportunity for children to perform for others if they choose. For a child with visual impairment, the provision of a barre, stable chair back, or shoulder to lean on can provide a sense of security in dance and movement activities.

Identifying instruments

Materials: Create a center with various instruments on a shelf and a screen large enough that two children can sit, one on each side, without seeing one another.

Supporting play: After children have had ample opportunity to explore the instruments, demonstrate how to play a guessing game by first examining and listening to several instruments, and then hiding them behind the screen. Have one child play an instrument behind the screen, while another tries to identify the instrument by its unique sound (timbre). To simplify, provide instruments with very different timbres. To extend the challenge of the activity, provide instruments with similar timbres.

(continued on p. 28)

Exploring bells

Materials: Provide a collection of bells of various types and sizes—resonator bells, tubular bells, handbells, jingle bells, and so on.

Supporting play: Encourage children to touch, shake, ring, and otherwise experiment with the bells. Extend the play by encouraging children to compare, contrast, categorize, and sequence the bells. Provide graph paper, blank paper, and crayons for those who want to document their findings. For children who have difficulty grasping the instruments, attach adjustable Velcro straps.

Musical theater

Materials: Transform your dramatic play area into a stage by providing costumes, instruments, seating for the audience, tickets, a microphone (real or pretend), and so on.

Supporting play: Introduce the concept of a musical show by showing clips of a videotaped concert, such as *Cathy and Marcy's Song Shop* or *Raffi on Broadway,* or segments of a video-taped stage production. Encourage

children to assume roles like ticket seller, audience member, actor, musician, and announcer. A guitar will probably be a popular choice. For children who have difficulty with fine motor coordination, a guitar pick is difficult to grasp. A rubber doorstopper is a good substitute for a pick and will produce a louder sound than a young child's finger strumming.

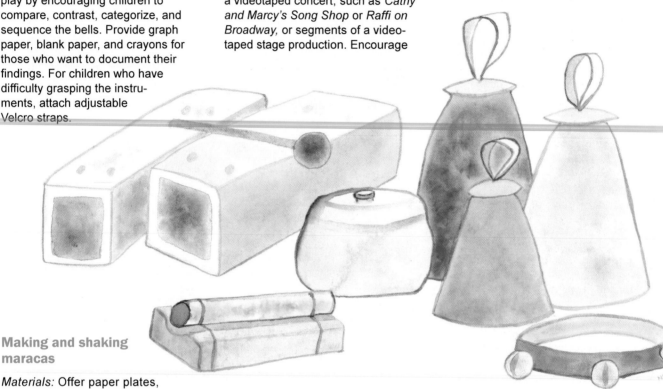

Making and shaking maracas

Materials: Offer paper plates, empty soda cans, plastic cups, pie tins, paper towel rolls. (Be sure the soda cans have no sharp edges.) Provide materials to pour inside them, such as rice, sand, pennies, small jingle bells, marbles, beans, and so on. Add a CD player and CDs with familiar songs.

Supporting play: Children can place their chosen materials between two paper plates or pie tins, then staple them together. Or they can fill empty soda cans, then put tape over the openings. Children can listen carefully and try to identify the materials in others' maracas. A children's marching band can play the maracas to accompany a familiar recorded song.

Exploring instruments from many cultures

Materials: Provide a variety of instruments from different cultures and countries. Remember to include instruments indigenous to regions of your own country. You might ask families to loan instruments and demonstrate their use, or inquire about borrowing instruments from music teachers or the music department of a local college. Include photos and perhaps maps (depending on developmental considerations) depicting the origins of each instrument. The Diagram Group (1997) publication *Musical Instruments of the World* may be a source of ideas.

Supporting play: Introduce the center and the instruments thoughtfully to ensure that children understand how to use them safely and respectfully. Allow children to explore and play in the instrument center two at a time. Guide children to compare and contrast the appearance and timbre (distinctive sound of a type of musical instrument) of different instruments. Children may enjoy comparing the different ways to change the sounds of various instruments.

Musical jars

Materials: Provide several identical glass jars, each filled with the same amount of colored water. Provide a striker, a small pitcher of water, and some paper and crayons.

Supporting play: Encourage children to experiment with the sounds made by striking the jars. If the jars are truly identical, they should all sound very similar. Suggest adding a little water to one of the glasses, then ask children to compare the sound made by striking that jar to the sound made by striking the other jars. You might prompt children to try to create a sequence of tones from low to high and then to create music or re-create simple, familiar tunes on the jars. Children can draw a picture to represent their composition or to show the sequence of the jars.

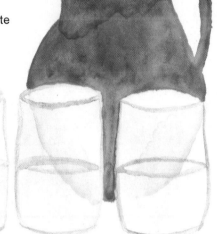

Recording sounds and music

Materials: Transform the dramatic play center into a recording studio. Discuss or read about places where records, tapes, and CDs are recorded. If possible, take a field trip to a recording studio. Then equip a center with instruments, tape recorders, microphones, and other recording props. Periodically change the instruments to introduce musical genres such as jazz, country, and classical. Offer markers and paper or software so children can make CD or audiotape labels.

Supporting play: Teach children how to use any real recording equipment before allowing them to play in the center. With the children's input, establish some ground rules for using the items. Encourage children to try out different instruments and record their sounds. After they play back the recorded sounds, ask children to think about whether and how they want to change their recordings. Prompt them to consider which instruments they want to play alone, which to play together, and how to time the vocals. This constructive planning and editing may require a good deal of teacher support until children are either satisfied with the finished product or simply satisfied with ending the process. Children can share completed recordings with classmates and family.

Playing different instruments

Materials: Provide one or two instruments per week in an instrument center—zither, child-size guitar, electronic keyboard, autoharp, shakere (gourd rattle), or whatever you have or can borrow.

Supporting play: Introduce the center and the instruments thoughtfully to ensure that children understand how to use them safely and respectfully. Model respect in your own handling of instruments. If you treat them like something very special, children will notice the aura of reverence. Allow two children at a time to explore and play in the instrument center. Observe carefully. If children get stuck on one way of using an instrument and/or leave the center after very brief exploration, they may simply be unaware of an instrument's potential. Engage in parallel play or more direct modeling to alert them to other ways to vary the instrument's sound.

Checklist for Creating a Music Play Center

Determine goals and objectives

Do your goals and objectives

☑ Consider the children's interests?

☑ Coordinate with the overall curriculum, school district/center goals and objectives, and related state, NAEYC, and MENC standards?

☑ Reflect the teacher's long-range goals for infusion of music into other domains of learning and development?

☑ Respect and reflect the importance of music as a domain in its own right?

☑ Encourage children to experiment with sound and investigate means for music making?

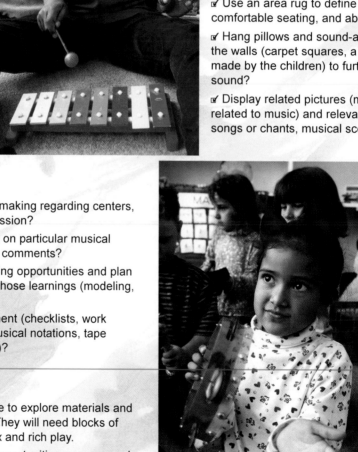

Define teacher's role

Do you . . .

☑ Include children in decision making regarding centers, using brainstorming and discussion?

☑ Encourage children to focus on particular musical elements using questions and comments?

☑ Consider the potential learning opportunities and plan a range of actions to scaffold those learnings (modeling, extending, adding props)?

☑ Set up a system of assessment (checklists, work samples such as children's musical notations, tape recordings, anecdotal records)?

Establish a schedule

Do you . . .

☑ Allow children adequate time to explore materials and construct musical concepts? They will need blocks of uninterrupted time for complex and rich play.

☑ Provide children extended opportunities, over several weeks, to revisit materials, practice with them, and engage with them in new ways?

☑ Allow children to interact with materials, both individually and with other children?

Create a setting and provide and materials

Do you . . .

☑ Use a divider or shelves to define the boundaries of the music center? Consider the flexibility a particular music center will have to mix with other centers. Clear boundaries help children keep music materials in the center and other materials out. Open up the boundaries to create more permeability and mixing of materials.

☑ Allot enough space to accommodate the number of children you expect will use the center?

☑ Position the center away from quieter areas of the classroom, such as centers for reading and writing?

☑ Rotate or add materials when the time is ripe to enrich children's play?

☑ Use an area rug to define the space, provide comfortable seating, and absorb excess sound?

☑ Hang pillows and sound-absorbing materials on the walls (carpet squares, a thick cloth tapestry made by the children) to further reduce excess sound?

☑ Display related pictures (musical instruments, art related to music) and relevant print (words to songs or chants, musical scores)?

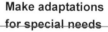

☑ Provide a small storage cabinet with a tape or CD player and headphones?

☑ Organize storage so children can put materials away easily and safely (Peg-Board hooks, separate labeled bins, a coat or hat rack)?

Make adaptations for special needs

Do you . . .

☑ Consider accessibility to the music center? Make sure all children can enter the center comfortably and access materials independently.

☑ Modify or adapt materials so children can use them in effective, satisfying, and safe ways?

☑ Consider grasp and fine motor manipulation as well as gross motor requirements?

☑ Address adaptive communication needs (for example, a communication board) for the music center as for other classroom areas?

☑ Consider structuring peer assistance through a buddy system, for children who might benefit from peer-scaffolded interaction with materials?

☑ Collaborate with an early childhood special educator and the child's parents if you need additional insight when planning your music center?

Encourage positive behavior

Do you . . .

☑ Plan the location of the music center carefully? Consider the possibility of an outdoor music play center.

☑ Move and rearrange the center when you change its musical focus and content (for example, it could sometimes be an outdoor center)?

☑ Engage the children in setting basic ground rules?

☑ Teach appropriate use and care of materials? Start with durable materials.

☑ Set and communicate limits for the number of children who can use the center at one time?

☑ Separate music materials from things that could damage them (food, water, excessive sunlight)?

Note: This checklist was inspired, in part, by ideas found in S. Moomaw's *More Than Singing: Discovering Music in Preschool and Kindergarten* (St. Paul, MN: Redleaf, 1997), 123–27.

Get going

These center possibilities are offered as inspiration, a starting point. "Checklist for Creating a Music Play Center" provides some suggestions of things to consider to enhance the success of your centers. Think about the purposes and possibilities of music in early childhood programs. Think about the musical concepts and attitudes that young children can develop. Think about the purposes and nature of play and the variety of ways adults can serve as scaffolders to accommodate the needs, abilities, and interests of a diversity of children. Then play around and get creative! Readers can invent their own ideas for music play centers and introduce children to the joys of music.

References

Andress, B. 1998. *Music for young children.* Fort Worth: Harcourt Brace College.

Berk, L.E., & A. Winsler. 1995. *Scaffolding children's learning: Vygotsky and early childhood education.* Washington, DC: NAEYC.

Bredekamp, S., & C. Copple, eds. 1997. *Developmentally appropriate practice in early childhood programs.* Rev. ed. Washington, DC: NAEYC.

Carta, J.J., I.S. Schwartz, J.B. Atwater, & S.R. McConnel. 1991. Developmentally appropriate practice: Appraising its usefulness for young children with disabilities. *Topics in Early Childhood Special Education* 11 (1): 1–20.

Diagram Group. 1997. *Musical instruments of the world: An illustrated encyclopedia.* New York: Sterling.

Dorman, P.E. 1990. The importance of musical play centers for young children. *General Music Today* 3 (3): 15–17.

Fromberg, D.P. 1999. A review of research on play. In *The early childhood curriculum: Current findings in theory and practice,* 3rd ed., ed. C. Seefeldt. New York: Teachers College Press.

Golden, K.M. 1990. An examination of the uses of music in selected licensed preschools in the state of Ohio. Paper presented at the meeting of the Music Educators National Conference, Washington, D.C.

Gordon, E.E. 1997. *A music learning theory for newborn and young children.* Chicago: GIA.

Isenberg, J.P., & M.R. Jalongo. 1993. *Creative expression and play in the early childhood curriculum.* New York: Macmillan.

Kenney, S. 1997. Music in the developmentally appropriate integrated curriculum. In *Integrated curriculum and developmentally appropriate practice: Birth to age eight,* eds. C.H. Hart, D.C. Burts, & R. Charlesworth. Albany, NY: SUNY Press.

Metz, E. 1989. Movement as a musical response among preschool children. *Journal of Research in Music Education* 37 (1): 48–60.

Monighan-Nourot, P., B. Scales, & J. Van Hoorn. 1987. *Looking at children's play: A bridge between theory and practice.* New York: Teachers College Press.

Moomaw, S. 1997. *More than singing: Discovering music in preschool and kindergarten.* St. Paul, MN: Redleaf.

Moorhead, G., & D. Pond. 1978. *Music for young children.* Santa Barbara: Pillsbury Foundation for the Advancement of Music Education. (Reprinted from 1941–1951 edition.)

Neelly, L.P. 2001. Developmentally appropriate music practice: Children learn what they live. *Young Children* 56 (3): 32–37.

Rohwer, D.A. 1997. The challenges of teaching and assessing creative activities. *Update: Applications of Research in Music Education* 15 (2): 8–11.

Stellacio, C.K., & M. McCarthy. 1999. Research in early childhood music and movement education. In *The early childhood curriculum: Current findings in theory and practice.* 3rd ed., ed. C. Seefeldt. New York: Teachers College Press.

Tarnowski, S.M., & J.R. Barrett. 1992. A survey of preschool music programs in Wisconsin day care centers and preschools. Paper presented at the meeting of the Music Educators National Conference, New Orleans.

Tsunady, M. 2001. Awaken the muse: Teaching music to young children. *Canadian Children* 26 (2): 8–11.

Promoting Creativity for Life Using
Open-Ended Materials

Walter F. Drew and Baji Rankin

"I just made a tulip and a sunflower. The tulip is not like a Van Gogh, but the sunflower is."

"I never knew toothpicks could do these things!"

"I need to get this big huge lump out of my picture. Never mind. I actually like it that way. I can draw a bigger flower now."

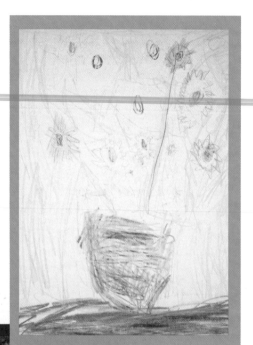

Creative art is so many things! It is flower drawings and wire flower sculptures in clay pots created by kindergartners after visiting a flower show. It is a spontaneous leap for joy that shows up in a series of tempera paintings, pencil drawings of tadpoles turning into frogs, 3-D skyscrapers built from cardboard boxes or wooden blocks. It can be the movement and dance our bodies portray, the rhythmic sound of pie-pan cymbals and paper towel tube trumpets played by four-year-olds in their marching parade, the construction of spaceships and birthday cakes.

What is most important in the creative arts is that teachers, families, and children draw upon their inner resources, making possible direct and clear expression. The goal of engaging in the creative arts is to communicate, think, and feel. The goal is to express thought and feeling through movement, and to express visual perception and representation through the process of play and creative art making. These forms of creative expression are important ways that children and adults express themselves, learn, and grow (Vygotsky [1930–35] 1978a, 1978b; Klugman & Smilansky 1990; Jones & Reynolds 1992; Reynolds & Jones 1997; McNiff 1998; Chalufour, Drew, & Waite-Stupiansky 2004; Zigler, Singer, & Bishop-Josef 2004).

Walter F. Drew, EdD, is a nationally known early childhood consultant whose inspiring workshops feature hands-on creative play with open-ended reusable resources. As founder of the Reusable Resource Association and the Institute for Self Active Education, he has pioneered the development of Reusable Resource Centers as community-building initiatives to provide creative materials for early childhood programs. He is an early childhood adjunct faculty member at Brevard Community College in Melbourne, Florida, and creator of Dr. Drew's Discovery Blocks.

Baji Rankin, EdD, is executive director of NMAEYC, lead agency for T.E.A.C.H. Early Childhood New Mexico. Baji studies the Reggio Emilia approach and is committed to building early childhood programs with well-educated and well-compensated teachers who find renewal through promoting children's creativity.

Photos © Walter F. Drew.

This article is based on field research, observations, and interviews about the use of creative, open-ended materials in early childhood classrooms and how their use affects the teaching/learning process. We identify seven key principles for using open-ended materials in early childhood classrooms, and we wrap educators' stories, experiences, and ideas around these principles. Included are specific suggestions for practice.

PRINCIPLE 1
Children's spontaneous, creative self-expression increases their sense of competence and well-being now and into adulthood.

At the heart of creative art making is a playful attitude, a willingness to suspend everyday rules of cause and effect. Play is a state of mind that brings into being unexpected, unlearned forms freely expressed, generating associations, representing a unique sense of order and harmony, and producing a sense of well-being.

Play and art making engender an act of courage equivalent in some ways to an act of faith, a belief in possibilities. Such an act requires and builds resilience, immediacy, presence, and the ability to focus and act with intention even while the outcome may remain unknown. Acting in the face of uncertainty and ambiguity is possible because pursuing the goal is worthwhile. These actions produce a greater sense of competence in children, who then grow up to be more capable adults (Klugman & Smilansky 1990; Reynolds & Jones 1997; McNiff 1998; Zigler, Singer, & Bishop-Josef 2004).

Children and adults who are skilled at play and art making have more "power, influence, and capacity to create meaningful lives for themselves" (Jones 1999). Those skilled at play have more ability to realize alternative possibilities and assign meaning to experiences; those less skilled in finding order when faced with ambiguity get stuck in defending things the way they are (Jones 1999).

In Reggio Emilia, Italy, the municipal schools for young children emphasize accepting uncertainty as a regular part of education and creativity. Loris Malaguzzi, founder of the Reggio schools, points out that creativity

seems to emerge from multiple experiences, coupled with a well-supported development of personal resources, including a sense of freedom to venture beyond the known. (1998, 68)

Many children become adults who feel inept, untalented, frustrated, and in other ways unsuited to making art and expressing themselves with the full power of their innate creative potential. This is unfortunate when we know that high-quality early childhood experiences can promote children's development and learning (Schweinhart, Barnes, & Weikart 1993).

The Association for Childhood Education International (ACEI) has enriched and expanded the definition of creativity. Its 2003 position statement on creative thought clarifies that "we need to do more than prepare children to become cogs in the machinery of commerce":

> The international community needs resourceful, imaginative, inventive, and ethical problem solvers who will make a significant contribution, not only to the Information Age in which we currently live, but beyond to ages that we can barely envision. (Jalongo 2003, 218)

Eleanor Duckworth, author of *The Having of Wonderful Ideas* (1996), questions what kinds of people we as a society want to have growing up around us. She examines the connection between what happens to children when they are young and the adults they become. While some may want people who do not ask questions but rather follow commands without thinking, Duckworth emphasizes that many others want people who are confident in what they do, who do not just follow what they are told, who see potential and possibility, and who view things from different perspectives. The way to have adults who think and act on their own is to provide them with opportunities to act in these ways when they are young. Given situations with interesting activities and materials, children will come up with their own ideas. The more they grow, the more ideas they'll come up with, and the more sense they'll have of their own way of doing things (E. Duckworth, pers. comm.).

Principle 2
Children extend and deepen their understandings through multiple, hands-on experiences with diverse materials.

This principle, familiar to many early childhood educators, is confirmed and supported by brain research that documents the importance of the early years, when the brain is rapidly developing (Jensen 1998; Eliot 2000). Rich, stimulating experiences provided in a safe, responsive environment create the best conditions for optimal brain development. The years from birth to five present us with a window of opportunity to help children develop the complex wiring of the brain. After that time, a pruning process begins, leaving

> Rich, stimulating experiences provided in a safe, responsive environment create the best conditions for optimal brain development.

the child with a brain foundation that is uniquely his or hers for life. The key to intelligence is the recognition and creation of patterns and relationships in the early years (Gardner 1983; Jensen 2000; Shonkoff & Phillips 2000; Zigler, Singer, & Bishop-Josef 2004).

The importance of active, hands-on experiences comes through in the stories that follow, related by several early childhood educators.

At the Wolfson Campus Child Development Center in Miami, program director Patricia Clark DeLaRosa describes how four-year-old preschool children develop some early understandings of biology and nature watching tadpoles turn into frogs. The fact that this change happens right before their eyes is key to their learning. The children make simple pencil drawings of the characteristics and changes they observe.

One day during outdoor play, the teachers in another class see that children are picking flowers from the shaded area and burying them. This leads to a discussion with the children about how to prepare a garden in which to grow flowers and vegetables. Children and teachers work together to clear weeds and plant seeds. They care for the garden and watch for signs of growth. Over time they observe the plants sprouting, leaves opening, and colorful flowers blooming. The direct, hands-on experience inspires the children to look carefully and to draw and paint what they see.

Another group of children in the same class takes walks around downtown Miami. The children then talk about what they saw, build models, look at books, and explore their new understandings in the block play area.

DeLaRosa describes a classroom that includes a number of children who display challenging behaviors. Some of the architectural drawings the children produce during a project on architecture amaze her. They demonstrate that with a concrete project in which children are deeply interested, and with teachers who guide them and prompt them with stimulating materials and related books, children's accomplishments can far exceed expectations. Because the children have direct and compelling experiences and multiple ways to express their thoughts, curiosity, and questions, the teachers are able to help them focus and produce, expressing their thoughts and feelings in a positive way.

When an architect supplies actual building plans of a house, the children become even more active. They make room drawings and maps of the house, all the while conversing and building vocabulary. They roll up the plans in paper tubes and carry them around like architects. Because the children are deeply involved in the project, DeLaRosa reports, they experience significant growth in critical thinking and creative problem solving. With questions like "How can we build it so it stands up?" and "Where's the foundation?" they show a

growing understanding of the structure of buildings and a deep engagement in the learning process.

Claire Gonzales, a teacher of four- and five-year-olds in Albuquerque, points out how open-ended materials allow children choices and independence, both crucial in stimulating genuine creativity. Children make things without preconceived ideas. When teachers support authentic expression, there is no one right or wrong way—there is space to create.

Gonzales describes a child who is fascinated by a stingray he sees on a visit to an aquarium. He is inspired to make a detailed, representational drawing of the stingray that goes beyond anything he has done before. Gonzales relates how he was able to use his memory and cognition to revisit the aquarium because the stingray made such a deep impression on him. The child recalled the connection he made with the stingray and represented the creature's details—the eyes, the stinger, the gills.

Key to this kind of work by children is the teacher's respect for both the child and the materials and the availability of open-ended materials like clay, paint, and tools for drawing and writing. Materials can be reusable resources—quality, unwanted, manufacturing business by-products, otherwise destined for the landfill, which can serve as much-needed, open-ended resources: cloth remnants, foam, wire, leather, rubber, and wood. (See "A Word about Reusable Resources.") Open-ended materi-als are particularly effective because they have no predetermined use (Drew, Ohlsen, & Pichierri 2000).

Margie Cooper, in Atlanta, Georgia, works with Project Infinity, a group of educators inspired by the schools of Reggio Emilia. She speaks of the value of seeing art making not as a separate area of the curriculum but rather as an extension of thinking and communication. Art making can be especially valuable for young children whose verbal skills are not well developed because the diverse materials offer a variety of ways to communicate. We can learn a lot from children who show a natural affinity for materials, gravitating to them without fear or intimidation. Cooper notes that adults often approach materials, familiar or unfamiliar, with apprehension. Learning from children's openness to materials is important so as not to teach children the fears or discomforts we as adults may have.

PRINCIPLE 3
Children's play with peers supports learning and a growing sense of competence.

Duckworth underscores the importance of this principle, emphasizing that by working and playing together in groups, children learn to appreciate not only their own ideas and ways of doing things but also each other's. A child can learn that others have interesting

> **B**y working and playing together in groups, children learn to appreciate not only **their own ideas and ways of doing things** but also **each other's.**

methods and ideas that are worth paying attention to and that can contribute to his or her interests as well.

In a kindergarten classroom in Worcester, Massachusetts, five- and six-year-old children study flowers together before a visit to a flower show. The children see and discuss with each other pictures of flowers painted by Vincent Van Gogh, Claude Monet, and Georgia O'Keeffe. They use some of these pictures as inspiration for their own sketches and paintings. They explore flowers with different colors, paints, paper, brushes, and print making.

To give the field trip a focus, the teacher, Sue Zack, organizes a scavenger hunt. At the flower show, the children work in small groups, searching for wolves, sunflowers, tulips, a large fountain, waterfalls, goats, a yellow arrangement of flowers, and a Monet painting.

At school the children make flower creations using recycled materials. At first, they have difficulty making their top-heavy flowers stand up. Then one child discovers that he can use the recycled wire available on the table to hold the flower upright. Others encountering the problem use their classmate's solution.

When children discover how difficult it is to make flowers from clay, one child suggests, "We can use the clay to make a vase and put flowers in it instead." So the project turns into making clay pots. Zack describes the children as being so involved that they seem unaware of her presence nearby. They are engrossed in their flower pots, expressing their thoughts to each other while working and using adjectives such as *smooth, bigger, huge, longer, taller, bumpy, dusty, sticky,* and *cold.* All the children are proud of their work, eager to show and share with one another. "Did you make yours yet?" "Where did you put yours?" "What flowers do you have on yours?" "I have a dandelion and tulips." "My flowers go right from a side to the bottom."

Here are children excited to be working in small groups and deeply connected to a sense of themselves. They do not look for external motivation or recognition. Rather, they express something direct and clear from within themselves as individuals. This is a wonderful example of endogenous expression, where children draw on their inner resources and express themselves from within.

Learning in a social setting is extended when children use diverse materials and symbol systems such as drawing, building, talking, making, or writing. The interaction among these various symbol systems—that is, different languages children use to express themselves—promotes and extends thinking in individuals and within the group.

Promoting interaction among these expressive languages fosters children's development and learning. And the languages encompass a variety of subjects, which leads to the next principle.

PRINCIPLE 4
Children can learn literacy, science, and mathematics joyfully through active play with diverse, open-ended materials.

When children play with open-ended materials, Duckworth says, they explore the look and feel of the materials. They develop a sense of aesthetics by investigating what is beautiful and pleasing about the material. The wide variety of forms of different kinds of materials, along with suggestions of things to do and to look at, flows over into artistic and scientific creation. These experiences naturally lead to conversations among children that they can write or draw about or make into books or other literacy or science experiences. Play helps children develop a meaningful understanding of subject matter (Kamii 1982; Christie 1991; Stupiansky 1992; Althouse 1994; Owocki 1999; Jensen 2001; VanHoorn et al. 2002).

The more children use open-ended materials, the more they make them aesthetically pleasing by fiddling, sorting, and ordering, and the more they see the potential in the materials and in themselves. "Knowing your materials is the absolute basis for both science and art. You have to use your hands and your eyes and your whole body to make judgments and see potential," states Duckworth.

Cathy Weisman Topal, coauthor with Lella Gandini of *Beautiful Stuff* (1999), points out that children develop power when they build individual relationships with materials. When children have the chance to notice,

> **W**hen children have the chance to **notice, collect, and sort** materials, and when teachers respond to their ideas, the children become **artists, designers, and engineers.**

collect, and sort materials, and when teachers respond to their ideas, the children become artists, designers, and engineers. When children are simply given materials to use without the chance to explore and understand them, the materials do not become part of the their world. Weisman Topal relates,

> When a child says, "Oh, I need some of that red netting from onions," he demonstrates that he has experience, knowledge, and a relationship with the material, a connection. It is not somebody else's discovery; it is the child's. Whenever a child makes the discovery, it's exciting, it's fun. The child is the researcher and the inventor; this builds confidence. (Pers. comm.)

Children's explorations come with stories, histories, associations, and questions. From the questions come the next activities, investigations, and discoveries. A natural consequence is descriptive language; children naturally want to talk about—and maybe draw about—their discoveries. "Not many things can top an exciting discovery!" says Weisman Topal. Organizing and dealing with materials is a whole-learning adventure. Working in these modes, the child produces and learns mathematical patterns and rhythms, building and combining shapes and creating new forms.

Teachers can promote language, literature, mathematics, and science through creative exploration. Margie Cooper points out that skill-based learning and standardized testing by themselves do not measure three qualities highly valued in our society—courage, tenacity, and a strong will. Yet these three characteristics may have more to do with success in life than the number of skills a person may have mastered.

PRINCIPLE 5
Children learn best in open-ended explorations when teachers help them make connections.

Working to strengthen a child's mind and neural network and helping the child develop an awareness of patterns and relationships are the teacher's job. Constructive, self-active, sensory play and art making help both children and adults make connections between the patterns and relationships they create and previous knowledge and experience. The brain, a pattern-seeking tool, constructs, organizes, and synthesizes new knowledge.

Teachers integrate playful, creative art making with more formal learning opportunities such as discussion, reading, writing, and storytelling. They ask questions and listen to the children so that the more formal learning activities are connected closely to the children's ideas and thinking. Teachers provide concrete experiences first: investigating, manipulating, constructing and reconstructing, painting, movement, and the drama of self-activity. Then the reflection and extension involving literacy, science, and mathematics that follow are meaningful. Zack in Massachusetts gives us a good example of this when she organizes a scavenger hunt at the flower show, encouraging children to make connections between their interests and activities at the show.

PRINCIPLE 6

Teachers are nourished by observing children's joy and learning.

A central tenet in the schools of Reggio Emilia is the idea that teachers are nourished by children's joy and intelligence. DeLaRosa clearly demonstrates this tenet as she describes teachers working with children on the architectural plans:

> Watching the teachers guide, interact, and work with the children makes me feel extremely excited—joyful just to see the gleam in their eyes. You know the children are thinking; you see them creating and producing and playing with purpose. I am proud to see teachers taking learning to higher levels, not sitting back festering about this problem or that. They could hang on to the fact that they have a hard time with some of the children . . . but they don't. They look at the positive and move on. (Pers. comm.)

A Word about Reusable Resources

Many of the materials used in art-making and play experiences can be discards donated by local businesses. Fabric, yarn, foam, plastic moldings, gold and silver Mylar, paper products, wood, wire, and a world of other reusable materials provide early childhood teachers and families with hands-on resources for creative learning.

Most businesses generate an abundance of unwanted by-products, overruns, rejects, obsolete parts, and discontinued items and pay costly fees to dispose of them. Throughout the nation, manufacturers dispose of their discarded materials in landfills and incinerators.

Through the establishment of a local Reusable Resource Center, high-quality, unwanted materials serve as much-needed resources for creative play, the arts, mathematics, science, and other creative problem-solving activities for early childhood education.

In this way businesses become a powerful force to improve early childhood education while reducing disposal costs, improving their bottom line, helping their community, and communicating a strong message that they are in business not just to make a profit but also to make a difference.

For information on Reusable Resource Centers near you or for training and technical assistance in developing a reuse program in your community, contact Reusable Resource Association, P.O. Box 511001, Melbourne Beach, FL 32951, or visit www.reusableresources.org.

Teachers and children learn together in a reciprocal process. The exciting work of the children inspires the teachers to go forward. Children are looking for more, and the teachers think, What else can I do to bring learning to the next level? How can we entice them to go further? What new materials can I introduce? and I can see how to do this! At times the teachers set up and move ahead of the children, and at times the children move ahead of the teachers. When teachers see what children can accomplish, they gain a greater appreciation for them and for the creative arts and materials.

In addition, the work that children do, while inspired by experiences teachers and parents provide, is at the same time an inspiration to all adults who notice. Sue Zack notes,

> The flower unit forced me to make the time to listen, reflect, and write down observations of the children. It felt good! It is what I need and what the class needs in order to be a group that communicates, experiences life, creates, learns, and cares about each other. (Pers. comm.)

PRINCIPLE 7

Ongoing self-reflection among teachers in community is needed to support these practices.

It is vital for teachers to work and plan together to promote children's creativity and thinking. By meeting together regularly over a few years, teachers connected with Project Infinity in Atlanta have developed the trust to have honest conversations with each other regarding observations of children and classroom experience—not an easy task. They are doing research and constructing knowledge together about how children build relationships (M. Cooper, pers. comm.). Just as children learn and grow in community, so do their teachers (Fosnot 1989).

Conclusion

Play and the creative arts in early childhood programs are essential ways children communicate, think, feel, and express themselves. Art making, fiddling around with bits of wood and fabric or pieces of plastic and leather, reveals the gentle spirit creating simple forms and arrangements, touching the hands, hearts, and minds of young children—and adults.

Children will succeed when they have access to a wide variety of art-making materials such as reusable resources, and when they are surrounded by adults who see and believe in the creative competence of all children and are committed to their success in expressing themselves. As we trust the process, as we encourage and observe the emerging self-initiative and choice making of the children, we come to more fully under-

This is my building. It is an office building. I made a lot of windows. People walk in the building and make money. They make money to buy something for money. Jonathan

stand the intimate connection between the spirit of play and the art-making process.

Given these optimum circumstances, children surprise and delight us—they create structures and thoughts no one has seen or heard before. We adults develop a greater appreciation for the children and for the power of creative art making and materials, thus providing a strong motivation for adults to continue teaching and children to continue learning in this way.

In this era of performance standards and skill-based/outcome-based education, it is more important than ever for educators and families to articulate the values and support the creativity of play and exploration as ways to meet the standards—and to go beyond them.

References

Althouse, R. 1994. *Investigating mathematics with young children.* New York: Teachers College Press.

Chalufour, I., W. Drew, & S. Waite-Stupiansky. 2004. Learning to play again. In *Spotlight on young children and play,* ed. D. Koralek, 50–58. Washington, DC: NAEYC.

Christie, J.F., ed. 1991. *Play and early literacy development.* Albany: State University of New York Press.

Drew, K., M. Ohlsen, & M. Pichierri. 2000. *How to create a reusable resource center: A guidebook for champions.* Melbourne, FL: Institute for Self Active Education.

Duckworth, E. 1996. *The having of wonderful ideas and other essays on teaching and learning.* 2nd ed. New York: Teachers College Press.

Eliot, L. 2000. *What's going on in there? How the brain and mind develop in the first five years of life.* New York: Bantam.

Fosnot, C.T. 1989. *Enquiring teachers, enquiring learners: A constructivist approach for teaching.* New York: Teachers College Press.

Gardner, H. 1983. *Frames of mind: The theory of multiple intelligences.* New York: Basic Books.

Jalongo, M.J. 2003. The child's right to creative thought and expression. *Childhood Education* 79: 218–28.

Jensen, E. 1998. *Teaching with the brain in mind.* Alexandria, VA: Association for Supervision and Curriculum Development.

Jensen, E. 2000. *Brain-based learning.* San Diego, CA: Brain Store.

Jensen, E. 2001. *Arts with the brain in mind.* Alexandria, VA: Association for Supervision and Curriculum Development.

Jones, E. 1999. The importance of play. Presentation for "The Play Experience: Constructing Knowledge and a Community of Commitment," symposium at the NAEYC Annual Conference, New Orleans.

Jones, E., & G. Reynolds. 1992. *The play's the thing: Teachers' roles in children's play.* New York: Teachers College Press.

Kamii, C. 1982. *Number in preschool and kindergarten: Educational implications of Piaget's theory.* Washington, DC: NAEYC.

Klugman, E., & S. Smilansky, eds. 1990. *Children's play and learning: Perspectives and policy implications.* New York: Teachers College Press.

Malaguzzi, L. 1998. History, ideas, and basic philosophy: Interview with Lella Gandini. In *The hundred languages of children: The Reggio Emilia approach—Advanced reflections,* 2nd ed., eds. C. Edwards, L. Gandini, & G. Forman, 49–97. Greenwich, CT: Ablex.

McNiff, S. 1998. *Trust the process: An artist's guide to letting go.* Boston: Shambhala.

Owocki, G. 1999. *Literacy through play.* Portsmouth, NH: Heinemann. Available from NAEYC.

Reynolds, G., & E. Jones. 1997. *Master players: Learning from children at play.* New York: Teachers College Press.

Schweinhart, L.J., H.V. Barnes, & D.P. Weikart. 1993. *Significant benefits: The High/Scope Perry Preschool Study through age 27.* Monographs of the High/Scope Educational Research Foundation, no. 10. Ypsilanti, MI: High/Scope Press.

Shonkoff, J.P., & D.A. Phillips, eds. 2000. *From neurons to neighborhoods: The science of early childhood development.* Report of the National Research Council. Washington, DC: National Academies Press.

Stupiansky, S.W. 1992. *Math: Learning through play.* New York: Scholastic.

VanHoorn, J., P. Nourot, B. Scales, & K. Alward. 2002. *Play at the center of the curriculum.* 3rd ed. Upper Saddle River, NJ: Merrill/Prentice Hall.

Vygotsky, L. [1930–35] 1978a. The role of play in development. In *Mind in society: The development of higher psychological processes,* eds. M. Cole, V. John-Steiner, S. Scribner, & E. Souberman, 92–104. Cambridge, MA: Harvard University Press.

Vygotsky, L. [1930–35] 1978b. The prehistory of written language. In *Mind in society: The development of higher psychological processes,* eds. M. Cole, V. John-Steiner, S. Scribner, & E. Souberman, 105–20. Cambridge, MA: Harvard University Press.

Weisman Topal, C., & L. Gandini. 1999. *Beautiful stuff: Learning with found materials.* New York: Sterling.

Zigler, E., D.G. Singer, & S.J. Bishop-Josef, eds. 2004. *Children's play: The roots of reading.* Washington, DC: Zero to Three Press.

Making the MOST

of Creativity in Activities for Young Children with Disabilities

Linda Crane Mitchell

In one corner of the preschool classroom, Nathan, age four, is exploring a tub of props related to the theme of community helpers. He discovers items typically found in a medical office—face masks, goggles, tongs, empty pill bottles—and pom-poms of various sizes and colors. Large white shirts hang close by where the "doctors" can find them.

After examining the items, Nathan, a young child who has a communication disorder, dons a shirt, goggles, and a mask. He picks up the tongs and begins to fill a pill bottle with pom-poms. He notices me sitting close by and invites me to join in. "Let's play doctor!" he says, while dressing me in goggles and a mask. During our 10-minute playtime, we identify the words for the items in the tub and try to pick up different-sized pom-poms with the tongs.

Our brief encounter during a creative play activity is an opportunity to enhance Nathan's communication skills and at the same time encourage his fine motor skill development.

Linda Crane Mitchell, PhD, is an assistant professor of education at Ashland University in Ohio, where she serves as coordinator of the early childhood intervention specialist program and teaches intervention courses to both regular and special education students. She has more than 20 years' experience in the fields of early childhood education and special education.

Creativity is the ability to invent or make something new, using one's own skills without the specific use of patterns or models. Creative expression develops through a child's participation in dramatic play, movement, music, and the visual arts. Teachers should plan daily activities that encourage the development of creative expression and meet the individual needs of children.

Inclusion of children with disabilities (cognitive, communication, physical, sensory) and specific learning needs in the regular classroom challenges all early childhood teachers to provide appropriate curriculum for children with differing abilities. Appropriate practices as defined by NAEYC are both age and individually appropriate (Bredekamp

& Copple 1997). The appropriateness of a program depends upon the degree to which learning is scaffolded for individual children—matched to the child's current abilities, with all the necessary supports to allow for successful completion of a task (Smith, Miller, & Bredekamp 1999). Thus, for young children with disabilities, the program should produce meaningful interactions within the early childhood environment (Carta et al. 1991).

Research support

Throughout the past decade research in education has emphasized the need for a more blended approach in preparing both early childhood and early childhood special educators (Miller & Stayton 1998). Early childhood educators must have the knowledge and skills to meet a range of needs and abilities within their classroom as well as possess a foundation of best practices and the ability to adapt curricula to meet the needs of children with disabilities (Kilgo et al. 1999).

The guidelines in *Developmentally Appropriate Practice in Early Childhood Programs* (Bredekamp & Copple 1997), published by NAEYC, and *DEC Recommended Practices* (Sandall, McLean, & Smith 2000) developed by the Council for Exceptional Children/Division of Early Childhood (CEC/DEC), support appropriate intervention strategies to promote the engagement of young children with disabilities within inclusive environments. Wolery, Strain, and Bailey

(1992) articulate important justifications for helping children with special needs to reach their potential.

Research has shown that young children with disabilities develop skills more easily if these are embedded in authentic play activities (Davis, Kilgo, & Gamel-McCormick 1998). This process is widely recognized in early childhood special education as activity-based intervention (Bricker & Cripe 1992). Modifications to the environment and curriculum activities are essential if children with disabilities are to benefit and make developmental progress.

Strategies promoting creativity

The use of the **MOST** (**m**aterials + **o**bjectives + **s**pace + **t**ime) strategies when planning curricular activities can help early childhood teachers plan more effectively for all children, including those with disabilities.

M—To plan creative activities, a teacher must consider the *materials* to be used and ensure that they will meet the needs of all of the children participating in the activity. By changing materials or adding special items, teachers make modifications to meet the needs of individual children. Materials may be modified for children with motor needs—for example, taping paper to the table during an art activity to prevent its slipping or adding larger size paint brushes to the art area.

O—Embedding *objectives* in creative activities can be accomplished by selecting specific IEP (Individualized Education Plan) objectives for individual children to work on during the activity. In the scenario about Nathan playing with a tubful of medical office props, labeling objects could be one of his IEP objectives. Natural embedding of specific objectives in creative activities encourages skill development within the context of play.

S—*Space* is an essential consideration as teachers plan creative activities. For children with physical or visual needs to actively participate, changes in the environment may be required. For example, planning for additional adaptive equipment, such as a wheelchair, may ensure a child's involvement.

T—*Time* is the final important element. Children who have disabilities may need additional time to actively engage in an activity. With this in mind, teachers

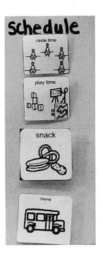

should make plans flexible so children have the time they need to complete activities.

A planning grid (see "Intervention Examples Using the MOST Approach") illustrates MOST concepts and provides a format teachers can use to plan further on their own.

Planning tips

Adequate modifications to creative activities are essential to encourage the participation of children with autism or communication, physical, sensory, or other specific learning needs. Following is a list of tips for teachers in planning for children with varying abilities.

Materials/modification of materials

• add pictures and visual cues to give directions and to use for communication

• label materials with words and pictures

• add props (real objects) to facilitate interaction and hands-on participation

• provide alternate items such as adaptive scissors and larger paint brushes that are easier to hold and use

• stabilize materials to prevent slipping or falling

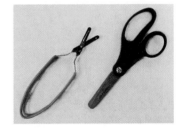

• model activities

• build in use of communication devices

• add tactile and visual stimulation such as bright, contrasting colors

• use other defining devices as assistance

• add scents to paints/playdough as sensory cues

• give verbal and written (visual) descriptions

Space adjustments

• create dedicated areas for specific activities

• use visuals to designate activity areas

• limit the number of children allowed to use an area at one time

- make sure there is adequate space for children's movement with and without adaptive equipment
- acquaint children with an activity space in advance
- provide movement cues with visuals, sign language, or braille
- add auditory and tactile cues when appropriate

Time considerations

- match the number of activities to a child's coping ability
- permit enough time for a child to become fully engaged
- prepare children for transitions with auditory/visual cues
- allow additional time for completion of activities
- require fewer activities

Intervention Examples Using the MOST Approach

Disability	Creative activity	M = Materials Modifying materials	O = Objectives Embedding objectives
Visual impairment	Pretend play	Use paint or colored tape to outline the edges of the furniture in the area to increase the child's ability to focus. Include bright-colored materials, large pictures, and large print.	The child will increase his or her social skills through participation in pretend activities with peers.
Hearing impairment	Music "Row, Row, Row Your Boat"	Incorporate the use of sign language into songs. Use songs that incorporate motions.	The child will use sign language to communicate with others during daily activities.
Autism	Visual arts "Sponge paint"—dipping shaped sponges into paint and creating pictures on construction paper	Provide plastic gloves for the child to wear during the activity (to manage an oversensitivity to textures). Make and display a chart showing step-by-step directions for the activity.	The child will use visual cues to assist in the completion of daily activities.
Physical (e.g., cerebral palsy)	Movement "The Freeze"— children move to music, wave streamers, and stop when the music stops	Attach a strap or piece of Velcro to the streamer to make it easier to hold.	The child will increase the use of the right arm and hand through participation in fine motor activities. The child will use a walker to provide needed support for movement during daily classroom activities.

Conclusion

Inclusion of children with various disabilities in regular early childhood programs challenges early childhood teachers. Literature throughout the past decade indicates that children with disabilities can acquire skills more easily if they are included in programs with their typically developing peers (Mitchell 2002). To effectively plan creative activities, teachers must consider each child's unique needs—ensuring that appropriate *materials* are used, IEP (Individualized Education Plan) *objectives* are embedded, and *space* and *time* are adequate. As a planning tool, MOST strategies can assist teachers in meeting the challenge of helping all children to benefit fully from participation in creative activities.

S = Space Adapting the environment	T = Time Providing adequate time
Keep the space consistent. Acquaint the child with the area in advance.	Build in time for the child to interact with peers. Use a peer-buddy system to promote engagement.
Seat the child close to the teacher during music activities.	Review the words (motions) to the song prior to singing.
Arrange the furniture so the child can work alongside or with a peer during the activity.	Follow a flexible schedule so the child has enough time to complete the activity.
Create adequate space for the child to move using a walker.	Increase the time when the music plays to support the child's participation.

References

Bredekamp, S., & C. Copple, eds. 1997. *Developmentally appropriate practice in early childhood programs.* Rev. ed. Washington, DC: NAEYC.

Bricker, D.D., & J.J. Cripe. 1992. *An activity-based approach to early intervention.* Baltimore, MD: Brookes.

Carta, J.J., I.S. Schwartz, J.B. Atwater, & S.R. McConnell. 1991. Developmentally appropriate practice: Appraising its usefulness for young children with disabilities. *Topics in Early Childhood Special Education* 11 (1): 1–20.

Davis, M.D., J.L. Kilgo, & M. Gamel-McCormick. 1998. *Young children with special needs.* Needham Heights, MA: Allyn & Bacon.

Kilgo, J.L., L. Johnson, M. Lamontage, V. Stayton, M. Cook, & C. Cooper. 1999. Importance of practices: A national study of general and special early childhood educators. *Journal of Early Intervention* 22 (4): 294–305.

Miller, P.S., & V.D. Stayton. 1998. Blended interdisciplinary teacher preparation in early education and intervention: A national study. *Topics in Early Childhood Special Education* 18 (1): 49–58.

Mitchell, L.C. 2002. Blending practices in regular education: A mixed-method design study on course practicum and training experiences in relation to preservice teacher attitudes and knowledge about inclusion. PhD diss., Pennsylvania State University.

Sandall, S., M.E. McLean, & B.J. Smith, eds. 2000. *DEC recommended practices in early intervention/early childhood special education.* Longmont, CO: Sopris West.

Smith, B.J., P.S. Miller, & S. Bredekamp. 1999. Using a combination of Vygotsky-based practices: NAEYC guidelines for developmentally appropriate practice and DEC-recommended practices. *Young Exceptional Children* 2 (1): 11–19.

Wolery, M., P.S. Strain, & D.B. Bailey. 1992. Reaching potentials of children with special needs. In *Reaching potentials: Appropriate curriculum and assessment for young children, volume 1,* eds. S. Bredekamp & T. Rosegrant, 92–111. Washington, DC: NAEYC.

Music from Inside Out
Promoting Emergent Composition with Young Children

Jennifer Ohman-Rodriguez

M usic has long been used to enhance the learning power of early childhood experiences for young children. Infants learn about relationships, love, and trust when loving adults share music with them (Jaffe 1992; MENC 2003). Toddlers and preschoolers learn the ins and outs of social interaction when playing rhythm instruments together. Teachers use songs and finger plays to ease young children's transitions and help develop language skills (Jaffe 1992).

Interwoven with these early childhood music experiences is music's capacity to communicate. Combinations of sounds convey, at the very least, concepts, emotions, ideas, and knowledge. Young children imitate these sounds to initiate and participate in music communication (McDonald 1979). Initially this communication is oral. But as with spoken language communication, teachers can lay the foundation for future music literacy by promoting emergent composition with young children.

The importance of music literacy

In early childhood, music's importance as a written language can be diminished or promoted. When promoted, emergent music literacy creates a path toward enlightened musical knowledge for young children. As with learning to read and write a spoken language, learning to read and write music allows young children to be music insiders. Lucy Calkins writes, "When children are insiders, they make connections" (1986, 219). Inside the language of music, young children experience music in profoundly different ways. They see the moving gears of music and the nuts and bolts holding it together.

What begins as music "exploration, imitation, [and] experimentation" leads to the development of connections such as "discrimination, organization, and creation" (McDonald 1979, 8). Being allowed in strengthens young children's use of music as a language and leads to new heights of awareness, ability, understanding, and possibility of communication (McDonald 1979; Jaffe 1992).

Emergent composition and symbols

As young children grow, so does their interest and awareness in symbols (McDonald 1979). The environment and adult-child interactions fuel this interest (Dombro 1992). Early uses of symbols occur at the art easel when children begin to paint faces, houses, and other important items (Smith 1993). Interest in letter symbols emerges when young children pretend to write by scribbling (Dombro 1992). Eventually, through their

Jennifer Ohman-Rodriguez, MEd, is an early childhood consultant in Davenport, Iowa, where her work focuses on the arts, grant procurement, and quality issues. Jennifer also has a bachelor's degree in music performance and continues to perform and compose.

interactions with symbols, young children discover that print symbols contain meaning (Dombro 1992).

In much the same way, emergent use of music symbols called *notation* develops. If the learning environment uses music symbols like it uses other written symbols, then young children begin to develop a budding music literacy. Playful experimentations with music symbols form a strong foundation for future music literacy, which will progress in similar stages to those observed in young children's use of invented spelling (Upitis 1991). Upitis describes the process:

> Just as the child in the precommunicative stage who makes strings of letters that don't form words, the child who plays with music symbols creates combinations that don't make melodies. (1991, 149)

> **I**nside the language of music, young children see the gears of music move and the nuts and bolts holding it together.

Sound is not important when young children first play with writing music. The sound picture is less important than the act of playfully writing music symbols. After experimenting with the medium of writing music, young children eventually stumble upon meaning in their compositions in similar fashion to their discovery of meaning in their artwork (Smith 1993). And with time, age, and experience, young children will decide before they begin what they will be composing, just like they will decide what to paint before they paint it (Upitis 1991, 1992; Smith 1993).

Music in the classroom

Young children need to be spoken to and read to long before they become readers (Dickinson & Tabors 2002). Young children also need to be exposed to music long before they become composers.

The foundation

Recorded music and rhythm instruments, as well as songs, chants, and finger plays, are staples in the early childhood classroom. Singing, improvising (banging around on the rhythm instruments), and appropriate background music provide a foundation for future music awareness (McDonald 1979). These early music experiences positively add to young children's sense of their musical selves.

Once a foundation level in music has been established, young children in their preschool and early

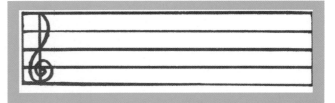

elementary years are ready for new levels of music awareness. Teachers can foster these new levels of music awareness by inviting young children into the inner workings (the nuts and bolts) of music. Once admitted, young children move from being singers and members of the rhythm band to becoming literate performers, composers, and critics in much the same way that children who listen to stories become writers and readers (Upitis 1991).

William Geiger

Becoming music insiders

To help young children become music insiders and emergent composers, teachers do not need to be musicians. Most teachers have already become, in a sense, biologists, anthropologists, and architects, not to mention paleontologists, so they can foster young children's curiosity, knowledge base, and investigations.

The nature of fine teaching enables teachers to still be learners and collectors of knowledge. Music, while out of the comfort zone for many, asks only that teachers have the desire to learn along with young children. One teacher suggests, "It's important for nonmusicians to remember that we are not expected to teach music, but we need to learn better ways to teach with music" (Sharron Lucky, quoted in Gharavi 1993, 28).

Starting out: Improvisation and recording

Improvisation and recording are great places to start, both for teachers and young children. Improvisation is the basis of composition as well as creativity. And for teachers who have little or no musical training, improvisation and recording are easy to implement, although noisy at times. Improvisations can be vocal or instrumental and begin as soon as young children are able to shake an instrument.

For improvisation and recording to be successful, the instruments must be available during free play. Availability allows for active exploration of the instruments and the sounds they make. Making tape recordings can occur any time young children are improvis-

> **M**usic, while out of the comfort zone for many, asks only that teachers have the desire to learn along with young children.

ing. Three concepts are important in recording young children's work: (1) children need to hear their work soon after it is recorded; (2) taped examples should be collected over time so that teachers, children, and families can note the growth and changes; and (3) tape recorders should be permanent fixtures in the music corner so that children can ask for their work to be recorded and learn to record themselves.

Teachers can use children's books to support and extend the concept of improvisation for young children. For example, Eric Carle's *I See a Song* is a picture book in which children can make up a song of their own to accompany the pictures. Young children's first attempts at using a picture from which to improvise may be hesitant or imitative of already known songs. Given time and familiarity, however, young children will soon take off with their musical interpretations of this book.

Chris Raschka's use of pictures, history, words, and word sounds in *Charlie Parker Played Be Bop* clearly depicts the improvisational nature of jazz for both young children and adults. This book explores jazz music and shows how jazz musicians improvise. In conjunction with improvisation activities and listening to jazz music, this book serves as a springboard to children's improvisational work.

The next step: Written music

Introducing written music to young children involves creating an environment in which examples of written music are accessible and experimenting with writing music is routine. It also involves promoting young children's discovery of music notation, the movement of music notation within a composition, and the understanding that music notation contains meaning.

Creating an emergent composition environment

Here are the first steps for teachers.

Create an environment full of printed music. It is a good idea to place books of music in the book area. Old and almost discarded books from piano lessons and the school band are good, plus books of children's songs. Children's books about music and music composers should also be available to spark further musical curiosity (see "Music Resources to Use with Children," p. 54).

Stock the writing area with beginner staff paper. Also include samples of real staff paper. Make sure to display large posters of familiar printed music on the wall. Posters can be either teacher made or copied and enlarged from existing music. When copying, choose a song in the public domain that is not copyrighted. (Copyright infringement fines are expensive.) Many children's songs are in the public domain. Public domain research can be done via the Internet or at a local library.

Set a music meeting time. Use one of the big music posters in the classroom to sing a well-known song, using a finger to help children follow along with the written music. Nonmusicians can do this activity by following the words. Young children will in time begin to understand that music is read in a certain direction and a note or notes is connected to each word. They may even begin to understand that when music sounds high, the notes are higher on the music staff.

Show children how music composers write music. At the next music meeting, start with a large piece of music staff paper. Large readymade staff paper available through music education catalogs is not expensive. While children observe and help, copy a well-known, simple song such as "Twinkle, Twinkle Little Star" to the staff paper. The important message for the children to receive during this activity is that composers write down their music on special paper (staff paper) and use special markings called music notation. Help the children to understand that they too can write their own songs using staff paper available in the writing area.

Bolster children's awareness of composers and their art. Reading Ann Rachlin's *Bach* at another music meeting will give young children an understanding of the experiences of real composers. Seeing pictures of the handwritten music manuscripts of famous composers helps children develop a knowledge of music notation and the process of composition.

Seeing pictures of the handwritten music manuscripts of famous composers helps children **develop a knowledge** of music notation and the process of composition.

Why and How Composers Compose Music

What motivates a composer? Many factors! For me and probably many others, the motivation for creating a piece of music is an emotional response to an event. It can be a tragic event experienced by many, such as the events of 9/11, or a deeply personal one like the birth of a child.

The process of composing is often seen as a cognitive function, but the motivation more likely involves emotion. Composers build relationships between motivations that are discovered, investigated, and shaped during the composing process.

There are many techniques for writing music. Some composers, including myself, hear part or all of a piece of music in their heads and then try to capture it on paper. I find hearing the music the easy part—writing it down is the challenge. Other composers hear music in a dream and awaken nightly to write.

Some composers improvise on instruments or with their voices and build a piece of music from part or all of their improvisation. Still other composers experience a certain rhythm that they just have to build a work around. Sometimes composers will practice writing music in different styles to challenge themselves musically. Text of a poem or a story can be an initial building block. Still other composers receive commissions to write a work for a specific person or organization.

Once a composer creates the foundation for a piece of music, he or she begins building the rest of the work. This process can be painstakingly slow or come together very quickly. Composers may create at the piano or at the computer. From the foundation onward, the act of composing is much like the activity in the block corner. There is a lot of experimentation, revision, knocking down, starting over, walking away, frustration (at times I've wanted to hit the piano!), and triumph.

Music manuscript pictures of J.S. Bach, Mozart, and Bartók are found in Aliki's *Ah, Music!*.

Introduce and name music terms. As young children's emergent composing continues, they will need more information about musical symbols. The treble clef, quarter note, and quarter rest all are fun to draw, and they mimic the lines, curves, circles, and squiggles of young children's drawings. Teachers can model drawing these music notations on large staff paper during music meetings, give each notation its proper name, and later add more symbols as the children are ready or at their request.

As young children continue to experiment, they begin to recognize and name music nomenclature. In children's emergent compositions, strings of music notes going any direction indicates their budding knowledge of music nomenclature. Notes mixed with pictures, letters, and words, and flagged notes with an overabundance of flags are also signs of this knowledge.

Schedule a performance. If they choose, young children can perform their own works as compositions emerge. Some may want a teacher to perform their works. Many times children make this request because they truly want to know what their compositions sound like. Nonmusician teachers may find a willing parent or fellow teacher to help play the new compositions. Making the extra effort to have an expert play the children's compositions is worthwhile because performance conveys a strong message to children that their works are being honored (Upitis 1991).

Young children's emergent notational skill and composition development grow and change over time.

Children gain new knowledge and insights in their progress through the stages of notational and compositional awareness. Emergent composition can become a staple of the educational experience of young children. Children's compositions will go from being sporadic experimentations with music notation to being real songs if the environment permits (Upitis 1991).

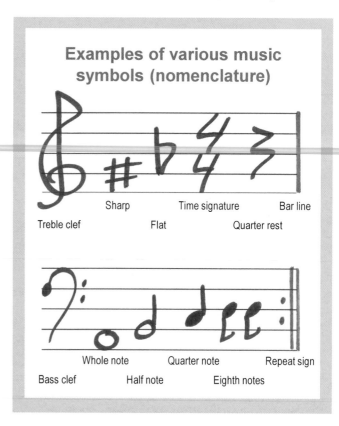

Examples of various music symbols (nomenclature)

Treble clef   Sharp   Flat   Time signature   Quarter rest   Bar line

Bass clef   Whole note   Half note   Quarter note   Eighth notes   Repeat sign

Music Resources to Use with Children

Picture books

Ah, Music! by Aliki. 2003. New York: HarperCollins. A children's resource book on the many facets of music, including written music and composers.

Bach, by Ann Rachlin. 1992. Hauppauge, NY: Barron's. The story describes Bach's life as a child. Part of the Famous Children series. Other composers in the series include Brahms, Chopin, Handel, Haydn, Mozart, Schumann, and Tchaikovsky.

Ben's Trumpet, by Rachele Isadora. 1979. New York: Greenwillow. A little boy who pretends to play the trumpet all day meets a real trumpet player.

Charlie Parker Played Be Bop, by Chris Raschka. 1992. New York: Orchard. A book based on jazz improvisation.

Frederic Chopin, by Mike Venezia. 1999. New York: Children's Press. Part of the Getting to Know the World's Greatest Composers series.

I See a Song, by Eric Carle. 1973. New York: Scholastic. A book in pictures that can be used to foster vocal improvisation

This Is Rhythm, by Ella Jenkins. 1993. Bethlehem, PA: Sing Out. A book connecting rhythms to everyday life.

Software

MiDisaurus, produced by Town 4 Kids. Provides an animated introduction to music. Suggested for ages 4–12.

Music Ace, produced by Harmonic Vision. Introduces children to music basics. It also has composing activities. Suggested for ages 6 and up.

Super Duper Music Looper, produced by Sonic Foundry. Helps children create their own music. Suggested for ages 6 and up.

Accommodating the needs of all children

In emergent composition there are many ways to accommodate children with special needs. Both auditory and tactile methods and mechanisms are available for working with children with sight impairments. Music therapy catalogs provide an excellent resource for exploring these options. A number of early childhood music notation software packages are designed for children. Some allow hookup to a special electronic keyboard. When children press notes on the keyboard, the software records them in standard music notation. Music software varies greatly in cost. Interested teachers will want to seek professional advice or help from local music store staff.

© Karen Phillips

Another adaptation, effective for curious toddlers as well as children with motor control issues, is punching out notes. Using a sharpened pencil, children punch notes into staff paper taped to carpeting or a computer mouse pad. The resulting holes can be read as notes and then performed. Other adaptive methods include using a magnetic music staff with magnetic notes, placing (and later eating) O's cereal on staff paper, or working with a readymade music notation felt board. Calling upon the expertise of other practitioners, such as music therapists, occupational therapists, and physical therapists, helps ensure successful experiences for all children.

The value of being an insider

As young children are given freedom to explore and learn to compose, music's door opens and they are allowed in. The mystery of a beautiful language is dispelled and replaced with knowledge. Introductions to improvisation, nomenclature, and composition give young children new tools for making connections and forming opinions

based on both preference and knowledge. Children connect many defining elements of music, such as melody, harmony, beat, and rhythm. In the process, they learn to value their budding abilities and their unique senses of self.

Inside music, a pathway to music literacy is established and honored. For young children, to be literate in any form of language, including music, is to have access to what is possible.

References

Dickinson, D.K., & P.O. Tabors. 2002. Fostering language and literacy in classrooms and homes. *Young Children* 57 (2): 10–18.

Dombro, A.L. 1992. Literacy in early childhood. In *Explorations with young children: A curriculum guide from the Bank Street College of Education*, eds. A. Mitchell & J. David, 161–75. Mt. Rainier, MD: Gryphon House.

Calkins, L. McCormick. 1986. *The art of teaching writing.* Portsmouth, NH: Heinemann.

Gharavi, G.J. 1993. Music skills for preschool teachers: Needs and solutions. *Arts Education Policy Review* 94 (3): 27–30.

Jaffe, N. 1992. Music in early childhood. In *Explorations with young children: A curriculum guide from The Bank Street College of Education*, eds. A. Mitchell & J. David, 215–27. Mt. Ranier, MD: Gryphon House.

McDonald, D.T. 1979. *Music in our lives: The early years.* Washington, DC: NAEYC.

MENC (National Association for Music Education). 2003. *Start the music: A report from the Early Childhood Music Summit, June 14–16, 2000.* Sponsored by MENC, NAEYC, and the U.S. Department of Education. Reston, VA: Author. Online: www.menc.org.

Smith, N.R. 1993. *Experience and art: Teaching children to paint.* New York: Teachers College Press.

Upitis, R. 1991. The development of invented music notations: A cousin to invented spellings. *The Journal of the Arts and Learning Special Interest Group of the American Educational Research Association* 9 (1): 142–63

Upitis, R. 1992. *Can I play you my song? The compositions and invented notations of children.* Portsmouth, NH: Heinemann.

Education Is a **Moving** Experience

Get Movin'!

Mimi Brodsky Chenfeld

Rain falls. Sun shines. Planets revolve. Earth turns. Fires burn. Volcanoes erupt. Gingerbread men run. Flowers grow. Clowns juggle. Frogs jump. Monkeys swing. Conestoga wagons roll. Flags unfurl. Ships sail. Archeologists dig. Wind blows. Continents shift. Peacocks strut. Tornadoes spin. Dorothy skips.

Verbs are action words. Participles dangle! Children are action nouns! They learn by doing. Children are action verbs! They're wigglers, bouncers, jumpers, movers, and shakers.

Sitting in one place for a very long time, sitting still marking worksheets or underlining words in workbooks for a very long time is bad for their health!

Thank you, Howard Gardner, for legitimizing movement, music, dance, drama, and play as basic ways of learning in your wonderful *multiple intelligences* theory that is now accepted by educators and philosophers the world over. We who work and play with children day by day and year by year have known forever that for so many people the most effective ways to learn, comprehend, absorb, *know* is through movement, music, kinesthetic experiences. Research supports the value of diverse learning methods. We're talking about making connections. It's all about helping children (and ourselves) see relationships. Learning isolated skills and facts in static settings is bad for our health!

The arts help us make the world whole. The arts are our oldest ways of learning, expressing ourselves, and communicating. Our ancestors painted masterful pictures on cave walls and crafted amulets, tools, and musical instruments that are preserved in the stones of ancient caves. Their paintings tell their stories. Animals were prominent subjects, but look carefully and you will see dancers and ceremonies and people caught in action. In many tribal cultures, there is no word for *art*. The arts are *part* of everything! Seasons, events, places, weather, life passages, community traditions—the arts are the core way people honored important ideas and happenings. Children learned their culture through the arts.

No matter what grade, age, or subject you teach, think *connections*. Draw a circle. In the center of the circle, in the hub, draw the children and the idea you want to convey. Draw many spokes (different spokes for different folks!). Write *dance, music, story, drama, poetry, visual arts* on the spokes. Don't leave out the standard curriculum areas, such as reading, math, social studies. All will connect to the central idea, to the children learning in their best, most successful combination of ways. And remember, movement, dance, music are very old ways. If your environment is one of trust and love, the words "show me" will be magical words that will inspire children to respond with bodies in shapes and motion.

During the 47 years I've been bouncing around the education field, we have danced and moved to depict

Mimi Brodsky Chenfeld, MA, in her 48th year in education, is a teacher, author, and consultant who travels the country to be with teachers, families, and children. Her many publications include *Teaching in the Key of Life* (NAEYC), *Teaching by Heart* (Redleaf), and *Creative Experiences for Young Children,* third edition (Heinemann). She is deeply involved in the education and arts communities of her home, Columbus, Ohio.

Reprinted by permission from the Houston Area Association for the Education of Young Children, *Advocate,* March 2003. Photos courtesy of the author except as noted.

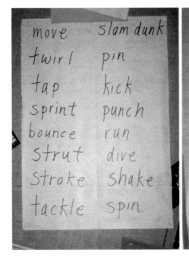

move   slam dunk
twirl   pin
tap   kick
sprint   punch
bounce   run
strut   dive
stroke   shake
tackle   spin

jitterbug   folk dance
reel
tango   pony
belly dance   monkey
salsa   mashed potatoes
riverdance   Detroit hustle
African dance   Cleveland hustle
slow dancing   monster mash

people escaping slavery and finding safety stations on their way to freedom; the galloping chariot of Apollo carrying the sun across the sky; all the king's horses racing to help Humpty Dumpty; the transformations of caterpillar to butterfly, tadpole to frog; the heaviness of molecules in cold fronts; the dynamic pageant of moving seasons; the wheels of the bus on the way to the zoo; number facts and spelling words; parts of speech and famous speeches.

Every idea is a universe of possibilities. Every idea, lesson, concept can be enriched by movement, by dance. Connecting movement to *all* areas of the curriculum, to *all* skills, is natural. The arts are the connective tissue that holds our spirits intact. Without the arts as part of our lives, we are truly handicapped.

As we believe, so we teach. If we believe that music, dance, poetry, chant, mime, and drama are a separate and sometimes unequal human activity having little relationship to anything else, that's the narrow message we'll transmit to our children.

If we believe that all concepts, topics, and themes have countless built-in dimensions of learning, we will help our children make discoveries, delight in surprise, and celebrate comprehension as they grow in awareness, knowledge, and skills.

All of our children are waiting, are eager to be invited to ways of learning that are joyful, meaningful, relevant, and multilayered.

On the way home from his preschool program, two-and-a-half-year-old Micah told his mommy about his morning.

She asked him, "How was movement with Mim?"

He said, "I helped Mim today."

"How?" asked his mom.

"I jumped!"

The children will help us remember what we know but sometimes forget: education is a moving experience! Get moving!

Thinking about Art

Encouraging Art Appreciation in Early Childhood Settings

Ann S. Epstein

ART APPRECIATION: **the critical understanding and knowledge-based awareness of the meaning and aesthetics of art.**

What is the place of art appreciation in early childhood programs? Can talking about composition, color, or technique with preschoolers ever be considered developmentally appropriate? Art appreciation seems like such an academic and abstract concept—the stuff of college-level courses. Surely it must be inappropriate to introduce an analytical approach to the arts to such a young age group.

On the other hand, who better to teach art appreciation to than children, whose senses and perceptions are so open and finely attuned to their surroundings? After all, the goal of art education is "to help children increase their capacity to create meaning and make sense of themselves and the world around them," (Smith et al. 1993, 3).

Producing their own artwork is one of the ways in which children create meaning in their lives. But they can also discover meaning in the art created by others and in nature. Such discovery is what art appreciation is about. Art becomes a way of perceiving and thinking about the world. Greater sensibility to visual imagery enriches human experience and creates new levels of understanding.

As early childhood educators, we don't ask ourselves whether language appreciation should pervade our programs. We automatically encourage children to express themselves verbally and to reflect on the words used by others. We want children to have fun with language, to appreciate its variety and its shades of meaning. Why should we not do the same for visual imagery—that is, encourage children to go beyond art's functional aspects and find satisfaction in its aesthetic possibilities?

This article promotes art education for its own sake. One reason we include art in the early childhood curriculum is that it enhances other areas of development, notably perception, cognition, fine motor skills, language, and social interaction. But lost in this approach is an appreciation for art in its own right.

Epstein and Trimis (2002) distinguish thinking *in* art from thinking *about* art. Thinking in art is the traditional approach to early childhood art: planning and doing art activities. Thinking about art, on the other hand, is art appreciation: reflecting on artists, artwork, and their meaning in our lives. While we engage children in

Ann S. Epstein, PhD, is the director of the preschool department at the High/Scope Educational Research Foundation, where she has worked on curriculum development, staff training, and research and evaluation projects since 1975. She has written extensively on early childhood development, staff training, and program evaluation.

> **T**hinking in art is the traditional approach to early childhood art: planning and doing art activities. Thinking about art, on the other hand, is art appreciation: reflecting on artists, artwork, and their meaning in our lives.

creating art, we should also connect them to the world of art beyond their own actions.

Putting art appreciation into historical perspective

Philosophies of art education change over time. In centuries past, the emphasis was on mastering the skills for realistic depiction. In the twentieth century, as photography took over that niche, trends moved away from strict representation. Over time there has been a "tendency . . . to give students—and most especially those who are young—great latitude in how they approach the visual arts" (Gardner 1990, 35). In schools art is now seen as a vehicle for promoting self-expression rather than a scholastic subject.

By going overboard in advocating for expressiveness in art, early childhood educators have made it anti-intellectual. "More than in any other country, art education in the United States has been considered an unimportant part of a child's scholastic profile" (Gardner 1990, 36).

Art, however, is as much an intellectual activity as an intuitive one (Arnheim 1989). Creating art requires perception, memory, and concept formation. It involves the use and transformation of symbols, pattern recognition, and the perception of similarities and differences. "Being able to think about something not present and then find a way to express it is a major cognitive accomplishment for young children" (Seefeldt 1995, 40). Understanding the cognitive basis of art development allows teachers to accord respect to art education and to see children's production of visual art as serious work.

Nonetheless, even those who value artistic development are apt to overlook young children's aesthetic development. Children have little experience identifying the elements of art (e.g., line, form, color, space) or the interaction of societal and personal forces that influence its production and interpretation. Early childhood educators fear that the study of art—also referred to as discipline-based art education—is antithetical to the position that art for young children should focus on creative expression. But is it?

Marjorie Schiller, a preschool teacher and professor of art education, maintains there is no contradiction between developmentally appropriate practices and the activities associated with art criticism and art history. In her experi-

Tying Art Activities to Children's Interests

Children's own activities and projects are the best starting point in art and art appreciation. To create art, children must first have a feeling, thought, or experience they want to express. Without meaningful and individual experiences, children tend to draw stereotypical objects. Following what captures their interests, children can observe and create with an artist's eye.

Stressing the importance of experiential and psychological motivation, Seefeldt (1995) cites an example of children in two kindergarten classrooms who were asked to draw a picture of a friend. In one class, children drew stick figures indistinguishable from one another. In the other class, children began by talking to one another about their likes and dislikes, their families and homes, what made them interesting and unique as individuals. When it came time for these children to draw a friend, they carefully rendered such personal details as facial shape, eye color, length and curliness of eyelashes, and so on.

The same motivation that applies to children creating art holds true for appreciating art. Arnheim (1989) advocates discussing artists' techniques in conjunction with a project that students have already chosen or willingly accepted. He notes that "anybody who has observed even young children spending long periods of time on some challenging piece of construction or deconstruction knows that there is no end to patience, once the goal is sufficiently attractive" (p. 33). Children will be curious about how artists achieve certain effects if they are interested in capturing similar qualities to represent their personal experiences.

The historical and cultural basis of art can also hold interest for children if it stems from their own activities. Arnheim (1989) cites a simple example: as children draw on paper, the teacher can introduce the idea that not everyone draws on paper. Some people draw and paint on bark. Children might then be interested in examining bark paintings (or works on clay, metal, and other media) and describing what they see.

Gardner (1990) also emphasizes that art education should be based in child-initiated projects. "Students learn best, and most integrally, from involvement in activities that take place over a significant period of time, that are anchored in meaningful production, and that build upon natural connections to perceptual, reflective, and scholastic knowledge" (p. 46).

ence, young children enjoy talking about art and identifying the aesthetic, personal, and social dimensions of artists and their work. The key, "as with any other area of the preschool curriculum, [is that] talking about art should spring from the interests of the children and be initiated, for the most part, by them" (Schiller 1995, 34) (see "Tying Art Activities to Children's Interests," p. 53).

Are young children capable of appreciating art?

Colbert and Taunton (1992), in a briefing paper for the National Art Education Association, identify three components of early art education: creating art, looking at and talking about art, and becoming aware of art in one's everyday life. While the first component is plentiful in early childhood programs, the second and third are neglected. Are children incapable of engaging in art appreciation activities? Or are such activities absent because adults have stereotypical notions about what young children can do in this area?

Research in developmental psychology (summarized in Gardner 1990) suggests that young children are more capable of art appreciation than we allow them to be. While very young children do not naturally focus on aesthetics, they display sensitivity to the quality of artwork if engaged in meaningful conversation about it. Similarly, preschoolers can sort artwork on the basis of style rather than its content if they are encouraged and interested in doing so.

Children can also think about and reflect on the artwork they see. If adults ask young children open-ended questions rather than teaching them didactically, children can offer simple analyses of what they think the artist is trying to say or how the artwork makes them feel (see "Language for Talking about Art").

Schiller (1995), for example, posted reproductions of fine artwork on classroom walls and made art books available to the preschoolers in her class. After giving children time to explore these materials, she engaged them in a discussion of what they saw and thought about the paintings. The children were fascinated to learn that Michelangelo painted on the ceiling, noticed in the reproductions the cracks in old paintings, compared Georgia O'Keeffe canvases to the flowers in their science area, and were surprised to learn that

Language for Talking about Art

The language of art is an expansion of the language of preschool. Both use terms like *color, shape, line,* and *size*—what Smith (1993) refers to as visual-graphic elements. Descriptive words such as *empty* and *full* and comparison words such as *lighter* and *darker* are used by children and art critics alike. In engendering art appreciation, teachers can help children expand the ways in which these common terms are used. Instead of focusing only on terms' *functional* aspects, such as clarifying that one wants the red cup, make observations about how features such as color evoke *aesthetic* responses: "The bright red dresses in that painting give the dancers a lively look."

Teachers can make children's art experiences meaningful through thoughtful dialogue. For example,

• Use descriptive rather than judgmental terms when talking about art. Say " I see . . . " or "it makes me think of . . . " rather than "I like it" or "It's pretty."

• After a small group art activity, encourage children to look at one another's work, and ask them, "Why do you think they look so different from one another even though you all made them out of the same paper and markers?"

• Introduce language to talk about the affect and aesthetics of the artwork. For example, "These colors look sad" or "All these little dots look busy on the page" or "This big, bright circle makes my eye keep coming back to it."

• Ask children to reflect on artistic intentions and feelings. "Why do you think this artist makes little pictures but that one makes big pictures?" is a question art critics studying the minimalist and abstract expressionist movements might debate. It is also a question that young children can ponder.

Connect children's natural desire to represent their experiences to comparable intentions of artists throughout the ages.

Writing, storytelling, painting, sculpting, dancing, composing music—these are all ways adults organize and make sense of what we know. Similarly, weavers in the Middle Ages wove great tapestries that depicted their particular understanding of nature, myth, religion, and everyday court life. Preschoolers have the same need as the rest of us to remember and make sense of what they know. (Hohmann & Weikart 1995, 225–26)

Conversations about art are important to this interpretive process.

> **P**reschoolers can sort artwork on the basis of style rather than its content if they are encouraged and interested in doing so.

Ninja Turtles' names were those of real artists. "The children instantly recognized that Matisse had a very different style than the realism of Michelangelo and da Vinci" (Schiller 1995, 37).

Preliminary accounts, therefore, indicate that young children can engage in art appreciation. They can regard artwork from the perspective of style and aesthetics, think about artists' intentions, describe feelings and sensations evoked by viewing works of art, and evidence genuine interest in the historical and cultural forces that shape the creation of art.

If we accept that children can do these things, we must then ask ourselves, How do we create the kind of learning environment and provide the kind of adult support that encourages art appreciation in preschoolers?

Including art appreciation in the preschool curriculum

Excellent resources describe how to stock a preschool classroom with art supplies, engage young children in exploring materials, and encourage the creation of art (e.g., Smith et al. 1993; Hohmann & Weikart 1995). Little has been written, however, about how to use children's creative experiences to develop a sense of aesthetics or a knowledge base about art. The ideas that follow are founded on child development principles, and they report the attempts of adventurous educators.

While the basic principles hold true, be aware that specific activities may meet with varying levels of success. As with all teaching, children may not respond immediately or in the way adults anticipate. And, as with any activities planned for preschoolers, be flexible and follow where the children's interests lead. But above all, don't be afraid to try.

Make sure children feel safe and secure expressing observations and opinions about art. Brittain (1979) notes that children must feel safe and secure to risk the challenge of

Photos © Gregpry Fox

producing art. The same holds true for sharing thoughts about art: children must know that their ideas will be respected and accepted. "It is important to accept a child's interpretation of what he or she sees, even if it is not the conventional view" (Hohmann & Weikart 1995, 322).

Sharing one's

© Gregpry Fox

response to a work of art is a public revelation about something highly personal. Children must trust their listeners to feel comfortable enough to reveal themselves in this way.

Bring reproductions and illustrations of fine art into the classroom. "Reproductions of the paintings, prints, and drawings of master artists are far more nourishing to children than Snoopy posters, Garfield cutouts, and cartoonlike images of objects, events, or stories" (Baker 1990, 23). The classroom can be enriched using prints, posters, photographs, and models, available at museum gift shops, bookstores, and libraries. Magazines and brochures feature reprints of work to be shown at upcoming exhibits. The book review section of the newspaper may contain illustrations from recently published art books. There are children's books about artists and their work. Families can save postcards they receive from friends and relatives who have visited museums.

Place these reproductions in locations where they relate to the children's interests and activities; for example, hang Mary Cassatt's paintings of mothers and children in the house area; van Gogh's paintings of sunflowers in the science area; junk auto sculptures in the block area; story quilts in the reading/writing area; Jackson Pollock's drip paintings in the art area.

Use art to establish a connection between home and school. Begin by learning about the art forms and materials in children's homes. Are there family members who create art and can visit the classroom? Does the art reflect other cultures or periods in the family's history? Mount exhibits of artwork brought from home, being sure to include both conventional and unusual media (painting, prints, sculpture, and photography as well as masks, weaving, pottery, calligraphy, beads, and baskets).

Use art from home to involve families in the life of the school and demonstrate the school's interest in family life. Similarly, encourage children to take home their own artwork and discuss it with parents and family members. Through their interest, parents can communicate that immersion in art is as valuable as mastering numbers and letters.

Connect children to art and the creative process in their communities. Use local resources. Visit artists in their studios and invite them to demonstrate in the classroom. Provide children with the kinds of materials and tools used by the artists they see. Take children on field trips to nearby museums and art galleries.

Describing a museum-based art appreciation program for preschoolers and parents, Piscitelli (1988) concludes that young children not only enjoy looking at art, but like sharing their joy with others. To follow up on museum field trips, children can stage their own art exhibit, recreating display cases, pedestals, and other exhibition props and spaces in the classroom. Engage children in making museum-style labels for their work that include their name, artwork title, materials used, and "artist's statement." Talk about where to set up the display in terms of lighting, space, and visibility. Children might further reenact the field trip by role-playing gallery guides, setting up a museum gift shop, or making ropes and other barriers to protect their artwork.

Observe art as it occurs in nature. Take advantage of aesthetics in the natural environment. Talk to the children about how changes in light (bright sunlight, cloudy day, sunset) affect the color of objects. Take nature

> **Y**oung children not only enjoy looking at art, but like sharing their joy with others.

walks, prompting the children to observe and comment on shapes and textures in plants, rocks, and wildlife.

In the classroom, look at examples of nature depicted in artwork and ask children to compare their perceptions with those of the artist. Ask what they think an artist found most interesting in a flower or rock or animal. How did the artist use techniques (size, color, texture) to draw attention to particular features?

Children are natural observers. By helping them consider what they see from an aesthetic perspective, you can simultaneously promote their appreciation of the natural environment and the artwork it inspires.

Conclusion

Teaching appreciation of art for its own sake is both possible and valuable with young children. Too often, early childhood practitioners limit art education to the making of art. But being artistic in the fullest sense also involves developing a sense of aesthetics. Enabling young children to appreciate art gives them another mode of learning through direct encounters with people (artists) and objects (the work they create).

By helping children grow from art producers to art appreciators, we deepen their understanding of the world and enrich their lives in the process. Few people continue to be art producers beyond childhood. But being an art appreciator is a skill and a pleasure that can last a lifetime.

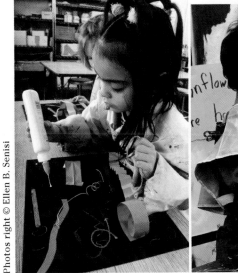

Photos right © Ellen B. Senisi

© Laura DeVault

References

Arnheim, R. 1989. *Thoughts on art education*. Los Angeles, CA: The Getty Center for Education in the Arts.

Baker, D.W. 1990. The visual arts in early childhood education. *Design for Arts in Education* 91 (6) 21–25.

Brittain, W.L. 1979. *Creativity, art, and the young child*. New York: Macmillan.

Colbert, C., & M. Taunton. 1992. *Developmentally appropriate practices for the visual arts education of young children*. NAEA Briefing Paper. Reston, VA: National Arts Education Association.

Epstein, A.S., & E.A. Trimis. 2002. *Supporting young artists: The development of the visual arts in young children*. Ypsilanti, MI: High/Scope Press.

Gardner, H. 1990. *Art education and human development*. Los Angeles, CA: The Getty Center for Education in the Arts.

Hohmann, M., & D.P. Weikart. 1995. *Educating young children*. Ypsilanti, MI: High/Scope Press.

Piscitelli, B. 1988. Preschoolers and parents as artists and art appreciators. *Art Education* 41 (5): 48–55.

Schiller, M. 1995. An emergent art curriculum that fosters understanding. *Young Children* 50 (3): 33–38.

Seefeldt, C. 1995. Art—A serious work. *Young Children* 50 (3): 39–45.

Smith, N.R., with C. Fucigna, M. Kennedy, & L. Lord. 1993. *Experience and art: Teaching children to paint*. 2d ed. New York: Teachers College Press.

© Elisabeth Nichols

Resources for Exploring *the Creative Arts* with Young Children

Books and articles

Amabile, T.M. 1986. The personality of creativity. *Creative Living* 15 (3): 12–16.

Amabile, T.M. 2001. Beyond talent: John Irving and the passionate craft of creativity. *American Psychologist* 56: 333–36.

Arts Education Partnership. 1998. *Young children and the arts: Making creative connections.* A report of the Task Force on Children's Learning and the Arts: Birth to Age Eight. Washington, DC: Author. Online: http://aep-arts.org/ PDF%20Files/Young%20Children.pdf.

Arts Education Partnership. 2002. *Critical links: Learning in the arts and student academic and social development.* Washington, DC: Author. Online: www. aep-arts.org/cllinkspage.htm.

Brickman, N.A. 1999. *Creative representation: High/Scope preschool key experiences.* Ypsilanti, MI: High/Scope Educational Research Foundation.

Bruner, J. 1996. *The culture of education.* Cambridge, MA: Harvard University Press.

Chenfeld, M.B. 2002. *Creative experiences for young children.* 3rd ed. Portsmouth, NH: Heinemann.

Cherry, C., & D.M. Nielsen. 1999. *Creative art for the developing child: A teacher's handbook for early childhood education.* 3rd ed. Torrance, CA: Fearon Teacher Aids.

Cherry, C., & D.M. Nielsen. 2001. *Creative movement for the developing child: An early childhood handbook for non-musicians.* 3rd ed. Torrance, CA: Fearon Teacher Aids.

Chosky, L. 1981. *The Kodaly context: Creating an environment for musical learning.* Englewood Cliffs, NJ: Prentice-Hall.

Crawford, L. 2004. *Lively learning: Using the arts to teach the K–8 curriculum.* Greenfield, MA: Responsive Classroom, Northeast Foundation for Children.

Csikszentmihalyi, M. 1990. *Flow: The psychology of optimal experience.* New York: Harper & Row.

Custodero, L., ed. 2002. Special issue, "Musical lives of babies and families." *Zero to Three* 23 (1).

de la Roche, E. 1996. Snowflakes: Developing meaningful art experiences for young children. *Young Children* 51 (2): 82–83.

Epstein, A.S., & E. Trimis. 2002. *Supporting young artists: The development of the visual arts in young children.* Ypsilanti, MI: High/Scope.

Fraser, D.L. 2000. *Danceplay: Creative movement for very young children.* Lincoln, NE: Authors Choice Press.

Froebel, F. [1826/1887] 1996. *The education of man.* Trans. W.N. Hailmann. Reprint.

Grand Rapids, MI: Kindergarten Messenger. (Originally published in London, England: Cambridge University Press.)

Gandini, L., L.T. Hill, L.B. Cadwell, & C. Schwall. 2005. *In the spirit of the studio: Learning from the atelier of Reggio Emilia.* New York: Teachers College Press. Available from NAEYC.

Gardner, H. 1993. *Frames of mind: The theory of multiple intelligences.* 10th anniv. ed. New York: Basic.

Gardner, H. 2000. *Intelligence reframed: Multiple intelligences for the twenty-first century.* New York: Basic.

Goleman, D., & P. Kaufman. 1992. The art of creativity. *Psychology Today* 25 (2): 40–47.

Head Start Bureau. 2000. *A creative adventure: Supporting development and learning through art, music, movement, and dialogue.* Creative adventure media kit includes guide for parents and professionals, videotape, and poster. Washington, DC: Author.

Hedden, S.D. 1991. Music composition with young children. *The Orff Echo* (Spring): 11–12.

Isenberg, J.P., & M.R. Jalongo. 2001. *Creative expression and play in early childhood.* 3rd ed. Upper Saddle River, NJ: Merrill/Prentice Hall.

Isenberg, J.P., & N. Quisenberry, N. 2002. Play: Essential for all children. *Childhood Education* 79: 33–39.

Jalongo, M.R. 1999. How we respond to the artistry of children: Ten barriers to overcome. *Early Childhood Education Journal* 26 (4): 205–08.

Jalongo, M.R. 2003. *The child's right to creative thought and expression: A position paper of the Association for Childhood Education International.* Online: www.acei.org/creativepp.htm.

Joyce, M. 1994. *First steps in teaching creative dance to children.* Mountain View, CA: Mayfield.

Kemple, K.M., & S.A. Nissenberg. 2000. Nurturing creativity in early childhood education: Families are part of it. *Early Childhood Education Journal* 28 (1): 67–71.

Levin-Gelb Communications. 2002. *Getting in tune: The powerful influence of music on young children's development.* Brochure. Washington, DC: Zero to Three. Available in English and Spanish.

Mayesky, M. 2003. *How to foster creativity in all children.* Albany, NY: Delmar.

Paley, V. 1990. *The boy who would be a helicopter.* Cambridge, MA: Harvard University Press.

Paley, V.G. 1992. *You can't say you can't play.* Cambridge, MA: Harvard University Press.

Pica, R. 2000. *Experiences in movement with music, activities, and theory.* Albany, NY: Delmar Thomson Learning.

Schirrmacher, R. 2002. *Art and creative development for young children.* Albany, NY: Delmar Thomson Learning.

Senisi, E.B. 2002. *Berry smudges and leaf prints: Finding and making colors from nature.* New York: Scholastic.

Smith, W. 2003. *Learning about music.* No. 3 of the Learning at Home series. Watson, ACT, Australia: Early Childhood Australia.

Thompson, S.C. 2005. *Children as illustrators: Making meaning through art and language.* Washington, DC: NAEYC.

Weikart, P.S. 1997. *Movement plus rhymes, songs, and singing games.* 2nd ed. Recordings on CD available. Ypsilanti, MI: High/Scope Press.

Weikart, P.S. 1998. *Teaching movement and dance.* 4th ed. Ypsilanti, MI: High/Scope Press.

Wheatley, M. 2001. *Leadership and the new science: Discovering order in a chaotic world.* Rev. ed. San Francisco: Berrett-Koehler.

Winer, K. 2003. *Learning about art.* No. 4 of the Learning at Home series. Watson, ACT, Australia: Early Childhood Australia.

Winner, E. 1982. *Invented worlds: The psychology of the arts.* Cambridge. MA: Harvard University Press.

Wolf, S.A., & S.B. Heath. 1992. *The braid of literature.* Cambridge, MA: Harvard University Press.

NAEYC resources and *Young Children* articles

Achilles, E. 1999. Creating music environments in early childhood programs. *Young Children* 54 (1): 21–26.

Althouse, R., M.H. Johnson, & S.T. Mitchell. 2002. *The colors of learning: Integrating the visual arts into the early childhood curriculum.* New York: Teachers College Press; Washington, DC: NAEYC.

Andress, B. 1991. Research in Review. From research to practice: Preschool children and their movement responses to music. *Young Children* 47 (1): 22–27.

Before and after school . . . Creative experiences. 1993. Video. Child Care Collection. Muncie, IN: Ball State University. Available from NAEYC, Spanish or English.

Burton, L.H., & T. Kudo. 2000. *SoundPlay: Understanding music through creative*

movement. Book and CD set. Reston, VA: National Association for Music Education. Available from NAEYC.

Chen, J-Q., ed. 1998. *Project Spectrum: Early learning activities.* Vol. 2 of Project Spectrum: Frameworks for Early Childhood Education, eds. H. Gardner, D.H. Feldman, & M. Krechevsky. New York: Teachers College Press. Available from NAEYC.

Chenfeld, M.B. 1993. *Teaching in the key of life.* Washington, DC: NAEYC.

Clemens, S.G. 1991. Art in the classroom: Making every day special. *Young Children* 46 (2): 4–11.

Cline, D., & D. Ingerson. 1996. The mystery of Humpty's fall: Primary school children as playmakers. *Young Children* 51 (6): 4–10.

Dever, M.T., & E.J. Jared. 1996. Remember to include art and crafts in your integrated curriculum. *Young Children* 51 (3): 69–73.

Dighe, J., Z. Calomiris, & C. van Zutphen. 1998. Nurturing the language of art in children. *Young Children* 53 (1): 4–9.

Edwards, L., & M. Nabors. 1993. The creative arts process: What it is and what it is not. *Young Children* 48 (3): 77–81.

Engel, B.S. 1995. *Considering children's art: Why and how to value their works.* Washington, DC: NAEYC.

Engel, B. 1996. Learning to look: Appreciating child art. *Young Children* 51 (3): 74–79.

Epstein, A. 2001. Thinking about art: Encouraging art appreciation in early childhood settings. *Young Children* 56 (3): 38–43.

Far ago and long away: Innovative storytelling. 1999. Video. Child Care Collection. Muncie, IN: Ball State University. Available from NAEYC, Spanish or English.

Feeney, S., & E. Moravcik. 1987. A thing of beauty: Aesthetic development in young children. *Young Children* 42 (6): 6–15.

Forman, G., & D. Kuschner. 1983. *The child's construction of knowledge: Piaget for teaching children.* Washington, DC: NAEYC.

Harris, T., & J.D. Fuqua. 1996. To build a house: Designing curriculum for primary-grade children. *Young Children* 52 (1): 77–83.

Healy, L.I. 2001. Applying theory to practice: Using developmentally appropriate strategies to help children draw. *Young Children* 56 (3): 28–30.

Hildebrandt, C. 1998. Creativity in music and early childhood. *Young Children* 53 (6): 68–74.

Howell, J., & L. Corbey-Scullen. 1997. Out of the housekeeping corner and onto the stage—Extending dramatic play. *Young Children* 52 (6): 82–88.

Hubbard, R. 1988. Allow children's individuality to emerge in their writing: Let their voices through. *Young Children* 43 (3): 33–38.

Huber, L. 1999. Woodworking with young children: You can do it! *Young Children* 54 (6): 32–34.

Jacobs, G. 2001. Sharing our gifts. *Young Children* 56 (1): 77–79.

Kirk, E. 1998. My favorite day is Story Day. *Young Children* 53 (6): 27–30.

Koster, J.B. 1999. Clay for little fingers. *Young Children* 54 (2): 18–22.

Lasky, L., & R. Mukerji-Bergeson. 1993. *Art: Basic for young children.* Washington, DC: NAEYC.

McDonald, D.T. 1979. *Music in our lives: The early years.* Washington, DC: NAEYC.

Mitchell, S.T. 2002. *The colors of learning: Integrating the visual arts into the early childhood curriculum.* New York: Teachers College Press; Washington, DC: NAEYC.

Moore, T. 2002. If you teach children, you can sing. *Young Children* 57 (4): 84–85.

Moravcik, E. 2000. Music all the livelong day. *Young Children* 55 (4): 27–29.

Music play: Bah bah, bebop, Beethoven. 1999. Video. Columbia: South Carolina Educational TV. Available from NAEYC.

Myhre, S. 1991. Caregivers Corner. With prop boxes we're always ready for creative movement. *Young Children* 46 (2): 29.

Neelly, L. 2001. Developmentally appropriate music practice: Children learn what they live. *Young Children* 56 (3): 32–37.

Neelly, L. 2002. Practical ways to improve singing in early childhood classrooms. *Young Children* 57 (4): 80–81.

Palmer, H. 2001. The music, movement, and learning connection. *Young Children* 56 (5): 13–17.

Roskos, K.A, J.F. Christie, & D.J. Richgels. 2003. The essentials of early literacy instruction. *Young Children* 58 (2): 52–59.

Schiller, M. 1995. An emergent art curriculum that fosters understanding. *Young Children* 50 (3): 33–38.

Schirrmacher, R. 1986. Talking with young children about their art. *Young Children* 41 (5): 3–7.

Seefeldt, C. 1995. Art—A serious work. *Young Children* 50 (3): 39–45.

Skeen., P., A.P. Garner, & S. Cartwright. 1984. *Woodworking for young children.* Washington, DC: NAEYC.

Smith, K.L. 2002. Dancing in the forest: Narrative writing through dance. *Young Children* 57 (2): 90–94.

Sousna, D. 2000. More about woodworking with young children. *Young Children* 55 (2): 38–39.

Szyba, C. 1999. Why do some teachers resist offering appropriate, open-ended art activities for young children? *Young Children* 54 (1): 16–20.

Wellhousen, K. 1996. Be it ever so humble: Developing a study of homes for today's diverse society. *Young Children* 52 (1): 72–76.

Williams, C. 1986. How do children learn by handling objects? *Young Children* (42) 1: 23–26.

Wolf, J. 1994. Singing with children is a cinch! *Young Children* 49 (4): 20–25.

Zimmerman, E., & L. Zimmerman. 2000. Research in Review. Art education and early childhood education: The young child as creator and meaning maker. *Young Children* 55 (6): 87–92.

Online resources

Americans for the Arts offers information on art education topics such as professional development, education standards, and research on art education and child outcomes. **www.artsusa.org**

Arts Education Partnership (AEP), a coalition of arts, education, philanthropic, and business organizations, promotes art in education. The Web site provides art education advocacy resources, information on funding opportunities, lists of AEP publications, and art education links. **http://aep-arts.org**

Best Children's Music.com offers easily accessible children's music, lists of musical books, research articles on music education and developmental outcomes, and links to music education Web sites. **www.bestchildrensmusic.com**

The Children's Music Web provides teacher resources—information on incorporating music into the curriculum, classroom songs, and links to other music education resources. It provides children with links to child-friendly music Web sites. **www.childrensmusic.org**

Institute for Early Learning through the Arts, a Wolf Trap Foundation for the Performing Arts program, provides professional development workshops for educators, creative arts enrichment programs for parents and children, and links to art education resources. **www.wolftrap.org/institute/index.html**

International Child Art Foundation (ICAF) offers educators information on the benefits of creative arts in the classroom and on art programs sponsored by ICAF, including international art festivals. The site includes artwork from young artists worldwide. **www.icaf.org**

MENC, the National Association for Music Education, advances music education by encouraging the study and making of music. Under Channels, find an early childhood network and forum and links to resources and information. NAEYC partners with MENC. **www.menc.org**

The National Art Education Association (NAEA) provides articles on child development and art instruction, updates on education policies, and information on its national convention. **www.naea-reston.org**

The National Dance Education Organization (NDEO) provides links to dance education publications, educational advocacy issues, NDEO-sponsored programs, and information on NDEO's annual conference. **www.ndeo.org**

VSA Arts, the coordinating organization for arts programming for persons with disabilities, offers arts-based programs in creative writing, dance, drama, music, and the visual arts. **www.vsarts.org**

Standards for learning

National Association for Music Education (MENC). 1994. *The school music program: A new vision—The K–12 national standards, preK standards, and what they mean to music educators.* www.menc.org/publication/books/prek12st.html

National Dance Association. 1994. *National standards for dance education: What every young American should know and be able to do in dance.* Hightstown, NJ: Princeton Book Company.

National Dance Education Organization (NDEO). 2002. *Standards for dance in early childhood.* Draft. Ed. R. Faber. Bethesda, MD: Author.

National Standards for Arts Education. *Summary statement: Education reform, standards, and the arts.* www.ed.gov/pubs/ArtsStandards.html

Reflecting, Discussing, Exploring

Questions and Follow-Up Activities

Marilou Hyson

The articles in *Spotlight on Young Children and the Creative Arts* represent just a small sample of the many valuable resources for early childhood educators interested in children's creative and artistic development. For students in early childhood professional preparation programs, for early childhood teachers taking part in training and other forms of professional development, and for individuals seeking to broaden their understanding of this important topic, we hope these articles and the accompanying professional development resources will open doors to this sometimes-neglected domain, which connects with so many other aspects of early development and learning and contributes so much to the joy of childhood.

To help you reflect on and apply insights from these articles, we have developed a series of questions and suggested follow-up activities. The series begins with an invitation to think about your own early experiences. Specific questions and suggested activities related to each article follow. Finally, we help you pull things together with general questions about curriculum, teaching practices, resources, and next steps.

Marilou Hyson, PhD, is NAEYC's senior advisor for research and professional practice.

A. Recalling your own early experiences

1. Do you now consider yourself a creative person? What early experiences contribute to your self-assessment as either creative or not creative?

2. What kinds of creative activities do you remember, in or out of school? Do you have positive memories of participating in those experiences, or are there some negative memories?

3. Was there an age at which your creative involvement decreased or increased? What factors may have led to the change?

B. Expanding on each article

"The Language of Lullabies"/*Alice Sterling Honig*

Why are lullabies beloved in all times, places, and cultures? Honig describes the many messages of lullabies and encourages caregivers to share these rich resources with children.

1. Reflect on lullabies in your own life. What songs sent you to sleep? If you are a parent, what lullabies did you sing to your babies? What do these memories tell you about the power of these simple melodies and themes?

2. Find time to talk with families about their traditional lullabies, and invite family members to share them. With their permission, you might tape their lullabies to use later.

3. The author encourages teachers to use lullabies or other restful songs to help older children relax and rest. If you haven't used this technique, try it for a week and note how children respond. Be sure to include Honig's suggestions about personalizing your songs with children's names.

"Sometimes a Smudge Is Just a Smudge, and Sometimes It's a Saber-Toothed Tiger: Learning and the Arts throughout the Ages"/*Resa Matlock and John Hornstein*

In this article Matlock and Hornstein remind readers that from prehistoric times to the present, the arts have always had unique power to help people understand and express their experiences and feelings.

4. "Humans have always used the arts to share and make sense of their deepest joys and fears." What examples come to mind to illustrate this point? You might think about books, films, plays, or musical pieces that have had this effect on you—either as a child or today.

5. The authors claim that early childhood educators should encourage young children to deal with disturbing or troubling parts of life through the arts. In your observations or in your work with young children, have you seen the arts (including the visual arts, music, movement, and pretend play) function in this way?

6. The box of suggestions titled "Creative, Arts-Based Activities for Teachers to Consider" has many ideas from the book *Project Spectrum: Early Learning Activities.* Select one new idea and implement it with a small group or with the whole class. What do you learn about yourself, the children, and creativity?

"Young Children Try, Try Again: Using Wood, Glue, and Words to Enhance Learning"/*Corinna S. Bisgaier and Triada Samaras, with Michele J. Russo*

The authors describe how a classroom project involving children in constructing wood sculptures can—with skillful adult support—promote many aspects of learning and development.

7. Many teachers have never included this kind of project in their curriculum. After reading this article, how would you explain to another teacher or a supervisor the value of a project in which children use wood scraps to create sculptures?

8. The authors emphasize that the wood sculpture project should extend over many weeks. Do you agree that it is important to devote considerable time to a project like this? Why or why not?

9. The article has many suggestions for teachers' use of language—questions, vocabulary, and concepts—to enrich and extend children's art making. Select one suggestion that is new to you, and try it out for a week. It may be something as simple as asking "Can you tell me about this?" instead of "What is it?" If you are not able to implement a wood sculpture project now, most of the suggestions can be used during other art activities.

"Books for Young Children about the Creative Arts"/*compiled by Sandi Collins*

The books listed here will introduce young children to well-known artists and to art forms including painting, sculpture, jazz, rock and roll, and tap dancing.

10. Select one of the books and read it yourself first. In making your choice, consider your own interests in the arts. It is important for children to see that their teachers have personal interests and a desire to share them with children. Next, consider how you might incorporate the book and its topic into an early childhood program. What related activities and experiences would make this book meaningful for children?

11. Read one of the books to a small group or, if it is more feasible, to an individual child. Share your observations of the children's responses at staff meeting or in your college class. What do you learn about children's responses to the arts? What might you do to follow up on children's questions and reactions?

"Music Play: Creating Centers for Musical Play and Exploration"/*Kristen M. Kemple, Jacqueline J. Batey, and Lynn C. Hartle*

Music does not have to be limited to a few songs at group time. The authors describe how well-designed learning centers can engage children in playful investigations of music.

12. If your program does not have a center where children can explore music during choice time, create one using the suggestions in this article. Note the recommendations about how to introduce the center's materials to the children and about the importance of giving children plenty of time for their investigations.

13. If you do not have an opportunity to implement a music center, develop a plan for such a center for future use. What basic materials might you include? What activities seem likely to engage children most effectively?

14. Enhance your ability to scaffold children's play with music by using one or more of the strategies listed in the article (plan, observe, participate, extend, model, motivate). You might make notes about how the children respond. Does their play become more developed? More creative?

"Promoting Creativity for Life Using Open-Ended Materials"/*Walter F. Drew and Baji Rankin*

In this article the authors present seven research-based principles and related concrete suggestions to guide the use of open-ended materials in early childhood classrooms.

15. What *are* open-ended materials? Why do the authors think these are so important for young children's education?

16. Find some open-ended materials at home and bring them to staff meeting or college class. With other adults, share your materials and spend time just exploring their many uses.

17. The article notes the joy that adults feel when they see children deeply engaged in play and the creative arts. When have you been inspired by the creativity and excitement of children as they make something wonderful out of open-ended materials?

18. Select just one or two open-ended materials (for example, cotton balls or fabric scraps) that are new to the children with whom you work. Over several days introduce the materials in the art area or other learning center, and then observe how the children investigate and use them. Consider what else you might add to deepen and extend their exploration: glue? Construction paper? String?

"Making the MOST of Creativity in Activities for Young Children with Disabilities"/*Linda Crane Mitchell*

Children with disabilities are included in many early childhood programs along with their typically developing peers. Mitchell introduces readers to what she calls the MOST approach (Materials, Objectives, Space, and Time) to planning creative activities that allow children with disabilities to participate fully.

19. The concept of activity-based intervention is at the heart of the author's recommendations. How would you explain and illustrate this concept for staff who are not familiar with it?

20. Hone your skills in using the MOST approach to plan activities for children with disabilities. On the planning chart (pp. 42–43), substitute a different activity for one that is listed. Work through each of the MOST categories to make this activity appropriate for a young child with a particular disability.

21. If you work in a classroom that includes one or more children with disabilities, implement your plan and evaluate the effects. Does the plan increase the engagement and participation of the child or children with disabilities? How do the children without disabilities respond? Describe the interactions between children with and without disabilities.

"Music from Inside Out: Promoting Emergent Composition with Young Children"/*Jennifer Ohman-Rodriguez*

In a rich musical environment, even young children may begin to understand and use the special language of music composition. The author describes how this understanding begins and how to promote children's musical literacy.

22. Like most readers, you may never have considered the possibility that young children would be interested in, or could learn, aspects of musical notation and composition. Having read the article, what value do you see in children's gaining these abilities?

23. The author compares emergent composition to emergent literacy. What are the similarities?

24. Following the author's suggestions, try involving children in improvisation (making up tunes, rhythms, or songs). Tape-record them to play back to children and to use in gauging the growth of children's ability to make their own music.

25. Make staff paper (specially lined paper for writing music) and include it at the writing table. Note the author's recommendations about waiting to do this until children have seen and shown an interest in sheet music and other compositional materials that you have made available and talked about. Observe children using the paper: what beginning attempts to create musical notation do you see? How does this change over time?

"Education Is a Moving Experience: Get Movin'!"/*Mimi Brodsky Chenfeld*

Mimi Chenfeld draws on her extensive experiences to remind us that "the arts are the connective tissue that holds our spirits intact."

26. Consider one area of your curriculum that could be enriched through dance, movement, and music. Why did you choose to focus on this area? How can you connect this area with other curriculum areas, program goals, or individual children's interests and needs. You might follow Mimi Chenfeld's suggestion and map the connections visually.

27. "Every idea, lesson, concept can be enriched by movement, by dance." Select one concept and with other adults, if possible, brainstorm ways that movement and dance could contribute to its development.

"Thinking about Art: Encouraging Art Appreciation in Early Childhood Settings"/*Ann S. Epstein*

Young children's senses and perceptions are open and finely attuned to their surroundings. In viewing artwork they can think about style and aesthetics, artists' intentions, the feelings art evokes. Epstein presents language for talking about art and tips for including art appreciation in the curriculum.

28. After reading this article, what would you say to another teacher who asks, "Why on earth would you include art appreciation in your curriculum? Shouldn't children just *create* art?"

29. Epstein emphasizes that talking about art—children's art or art made by others—is a great way to develop vocabulary. You might spend a week intentionally introducing rich ways to describe artistic creations and asking questions that promote children's use of new words and elaborated language.

30. This article suggests a number of ways to get started with art appreciation. They include a museum field trip with follow-up activities, a classroom exhibit of artwork by family members, and the use of postcard reproductions of famous paintings to stimulate observation and discussion. Try one of these suggestions and evaluate children's responses.

C. Making connections

Consider the big picture

1. What, in your view, are the three most important themes or key ideas that recur in this collection of articles? If possible, compare your nominations with those identified by other readers.

2. Again, thinking of the entire group of articles, what are three key teacher behaviors that support young children's involvement and growth in the creative arts? And what are three aspects of the classroom environment that do the same?

3. Because this is a small collection of articles, some important ideas may have been left out or under-represented. What topics would you add? Where might you learn more about these missing pieces?

Examine curriculum goals and expected outcomes

4. Review "Early Childhood Curriculum, Assessment, and Program Evaluation," the joint position statement of NAEYC and the National Association of Early Childhood Specialists in State Departments of Education (NAECS/SDE)(find it online at www.naeyc .org/about/positions/pdf/pscape.pdf). How are the recommendations in this Spotlight book similar to those in the position statement?

5. Depending on the ages of the children with whom you work and the program setting, review (a) the state early learning standards (check the Web site of your state department of education), (b) the Head Start Child Outcomes Framework (www.hsnrc. org/CDI/pdfs/UGCOF.pdf), or (c) the relevant section of your state's K–12 standards (again, you will find them on your state department of education's Web site). Are the creative arts represented in these standards? If so, do the standards emphasize the aspects of the arts that the authors of these articles consider important?

6. If your program uses a particular curriculum, examine it to see how the creative arts are adressed. What seem to be the goals of the curriculum in relation to the creative arts? What types of creative activities are recommended, and why?

7. Review one or more of the national standards for learning for music, dance, or the arts that are listed in the resource section of this book (see "Standards for Learning," p. 59). How does your program's curriculum reflect the standards? What changes are needed?

Use reflection to enhance teaching practices

8. As you read and discuss the entire set of articles, what do you find that affirms your current practices? What questions do these articles raise about your current practices? What new approaches might you try?

9. Many of these articles include information from research and other sources documenting the positive influence of the creative arts, play, and exploration on children's future development and learning. Using some of these points, work alone or as a group to create a poster that communicates these ideas in words and vivid images.

10. Conduct focused observations of creative behavior. You might choose one child to observe—perhaps a child whom you have not thought of as creative. Over several days or weeks, note the child's involvement with open-ended materials, music and movement, drawing and painting, and playful exploration of all kinds. What types of experiences seem to be most engaging for this child? And how might you enhance those experiences to add to the child's opportunities to experience and express creativity?

11. Take photographs of children at moments of creative involvement. Portray a wide array of experiences and experiments. Then use the photographs in a display, with accompanying descriptions of what the children are doing and what they are learning in the process. Share the display with colleagues, fellow students, families.

12. Select one area of your classroom, family child care home, or outdoor playground and consider ways to use this area to foster children's involvement in the creative arts. For example, might children write and illustrate their own books if you added blank "books" with crayons, markers, and pencils to the book area? If you put a basket of colorful streamers next to the climber, would some children tie and wrap the poles in beautiful patterns? Try a few ideas and observe the results.

13. Give yourself time to explore a new area of the creative arts simply for your own enjoyment. You

could take a dance class, try your hand at water-color painting, or make a collage of photographs for a friend who is moving away. Whatever you try, stick with it long enough to experience the enjoyment of self-expression and exploration. What do these insights tell you about young children's involvement in the creative arts?

14. In your opinion, what is creativity? Write your own definition and compare it with the definitions written by your colleagues or fellow students. Then review the articles in this book and see how various authors have defined the concept. How have your ideas about creativity, the creative arts, and the creative process changed as a result of reading, reflecting, and acting upon these articles?

Focus on families and communities

15. Some families may see the creative arts as "frills" that distract children from learning to read, write, and be academically successful. Other families may consider them to be important but may expect children to produce accurate representations or to follow teacher-produced models. Using the information in these articles, how might you help all families support their children's creativity while respecting their concerns, hopes, and dreams?

16. Develop a plan for a Creative Family Night when families could look at their children's drawings, listen to recordings of their musical improvisations, see videos of their movement explorations—and perhaps try some creative activities themselves.

17. If you are currently teaching young children, try to learn more about parents' or grandparents' involvement in the creative arts. Perhaps family members can share their joy and expertise with the children—whether knitting beautiful patterns, playing the accordion, or performing traditional dances.

18. How can you help families gain greater insight into the beauty and wonder of children's creations? Besides sending children's work home, you could develop displays or documentation panels that pair

photos of children's activities with their responses to "Tell me about what you made" questions, as well as brief descriptions, written by you, of what the drawings and paintings reveal about how the children look at and represent the world.

Identify resources and plan next steps

19. Besides the resources at the end of each article, this book offers "Resources for Exploring the Creative Arts with Young Children" (pp. 58–59), a list of books, articles, online resources, and national standards related to the creative arts in early childhood. Select one or more of the resources, read the selection, and create an annotated description or review to guide others—perhaps putting the information into handouts or creating a Web resource. What is the early childhood content? Who is the audience? What are some uses of the material? For which professionals or groups of children is the resource especially valuable?

20. In addition to the resources in this book, what others have you found to support your work on young children's creative expression and involvement in the arts? Again, you might create an annotated list to share.

21. What do you feel you need to learn in order to support children's creative development and to use the arts to support learning in other areas? As you read the articles, what gaps did you find in your own understanding, and how might you fill those gaps? What will you want to change (for example, in your classroom, your schedule, some aspects of teaching practices) in order to support children's creative expression and involvement in the arts?

22. Develop specific plans to engage children in a variety of creative arts experiences that will build their confidence, joy, and breadth of understanding. Develop an action plan to guide this work. Implement your plans and record what happens through observation notes, journal entries, video, or photos.